RECONCILIATION

The Path to Inner Peace

RECONCILIATION

The Path to Inner Peace

MARISAH LITEZEN

Reconciliation
The Path to Inner Peace

Copyright ©2019 by Marisah Litezen
All rights reserved.
Book cover design by Paul Melecky

Published by Next Century Publishing
Austin, TX
www.NextCenturyPublishing.com

No part of this publication may be reproduced, stored in a retrieval system, or transmitted in any form or by any means—electronic, mechanical, photocopy, recording, or any other—without the prior permission of the author.

ISBN: 978-1-68102-953-5

Printed in the United States of America

ACKNOWLEDGEMENT

Special thanks to my maternal grandmother and my parents for raising me "Fran Ginen"; to brother Malik for planting the seed of Liberation in my mind; to my family for believing in me; to my sister, L., for her positive influence on my spiritual development; to the staff of Next Century Publishing for their professional assistance, principally Michael Kopp, Leslie Garcia, Simon Presland and Mike Owens; to Eugenia and Paul Melecky for the book cover illustration. I would like to especially thank my husband D. for sharing his wealth of information with me. A heartful acknowledgement goes to my son, Q. for the inside illustrations and all his feedback, particularly involving the intro of this book.

CONTENTS

Foreword 1
Introduction 3

RECONCILIATION
The Caldron 9

THE MATHEMATICS
The Tenth Department 13
Five Percent In The Tenth 21

ANOTHER REALITY
A Native's Spiritual Narrative 29

THE AUSARIAN EXPERIENCE
The Neteru 39
The Story Of Ausar 49
A Path With A Heart 51

THE RETURN OF HERU

Heru 57
The Catholic Experience......................................61
Voodoo 67

RECONCILIATION

The *I Ching*..73
Awareness A Brief Discussion 77
The Channeling Of Energy 79
Demystification...87
Conclusion..91

RECONCILIATION

The Path to Inner Peace

FOREWORD

This book tracks my personal experience of reconciliation. I decided to write it because I believe it can help readers find a common ground amongst diverse views and explanations regarding the human experience on Earth. I also hope that the message it conveys becomes epidemically inspiring for the achievement of inner peace. *Reconciliation* describes my individual evolution into adulthood by means of studying certain world perspectives including Voodoo and Shamanism. My interaction with these philosophical worldviews initialized themselves in various ways including accidentally, coincidentally, intentionally, and inevitably. Whatever the circumstance, by practicing some inspirational prescriptions of these universal precepts, I began to truly understand our individual responsibility to improve the way we live. As I learned about alternative interpretations of the human experience in the world, a lock clicked open inside of me. I found a key that I believe, reveals a source of peace for humankind. I feel compelled to share this revelation without any claim of veneration (for myself), if indeed I succeed in my quest to touch as many individuals as possible.

INTRODUCTION

Our personal understanding or perception of the world is strongly rooted in the moment of our conception. We are fundamentally the product of our parents' social interactions with each other. Times of mutual amicability and discord affect the quality of their intimate encounters and the intensity level of their coupling instances. The degree of sensual stimulation and sexual arousal during the precise moment we are conceived infuses the bearing of our inevitable life on earth. From that time on, we begin to acquire an impression of our environment including the place, the time, the people, and their culture. Most importantly, we just become a receptacle of human emotions (joy, anger, happiness, sadness…) and environmental emissions (smells, sounds, tastes, touch…). We will be affected for better or for worse until the opportune day when we've matured physiologically enough to exit the maternal matrix.

Once in the cradle, we are able to interact directly with our environment. We now can see, or sense people, objects, and events around us. During this first stage of our earthly existence, we're still for the most part subjected to people's feelings and actions as well as external occurrences such as brightness, darkness, loudness, quietness, cold, heat, dryness, wetness… Our awareness of the world, however, continues to expand. We begin to observe more, to learn, and to remember. Thereon, under adequate settings and conditions (presuming our own physical, mental, and psychological health) we develop the ability to express personal emotions and display patterns of learned behavior in responses to environmental stimulations.

Parents, guardians, caretakers, and other people incessantly feed us ideas that nourish our conception of the world and greatly contribute to our development through time. Using spoken, body, and sign languages, they communicate to us their interpretations of life events. They teach us traditions, moral values, and social norms. They expose our senses to situations such as celebrations, rituals, games, songs, and much more to mold and reinforce our view of physical reality. They proceed to show us how to use objects around us such as utensils, tools, and furniture. They also teach us about the consumption of edible plants, fruits, and other food items. Thus, we become acculturated.

The more we internalize the concepts we learn, the scenes we witness, and all the experiences we go through, the more we develop patterns of behavior or habits that connect us to the milieu of our infancy within a traditional family unit (with mom, dad, and siblings), an orphanage, a foster home, or other types of household. During that time, we acquire the fundamentals of a belief system collective to the society where we pertain and grow in age.

As we develop towards adulthood, other people including school teachers, relatives, siblings, religious leaders, friends…proceed to teach us more complex concepts and intricate ideas, which further stimulate our mental ability to follow appropriate models of behavior into maturity. We become increasingly conditioned to act, react, and interact according to generally accepted social conduct in our environment. This life process contributes to reinforce our cultural identity rooted in the depth of our collective belief system. For instance, I was born in Ayiti,*[1] an Antillean country. Therefore, I partake to its people's way of life and cultural expressions. Like most Ayisyens, I received a formal Christian education. In my youth, I attended Catholic schools. I received the rites of Baptism, First Communion, and Confirmation. Within the confines of traditional

---

1   According to some historians, during Pre-Columbian era, the natives who inhabited the island comprising today's Haiti and the Dominican Republic, called the land Ayiti, Quiskeya or Bohio.

ground however, I learned to associate Catholic Saints to specific aspects of the Divine. To that effect, I remember a song my mom used to sing at times. The words are evidently in Creole (a mixture of African languages, French, Spanish, and English):

	(English Translation)
Nape mande kouman nou ye. (bis)	*We are asking how you're doing.*
Men wi nou la (bis),	*We are just fine,*
Dambala Wedo.	*Dambala Wedo.*
La vi nou lan men Bon Dye.	*Our life is in God's hands.*
Nape mande kouman nou ye (bis)	*We are asking how you're doing.*
Men wi nou la, (bis).	*We are just fine,*
Ayida Wedo.	*Ayida Wedo.*
La vi nou lan men Bon Dye.	*Our life is in God's hands.*

In Voodoo, Dambala Wedo and Ayida Wedo are male and female complementary manifestations of the Divine energy. "Damballah and Ayida, who together represent the sexual totality, encompass the cosmos as a serpent coiled about the world." (Divine Horsemen, p. 116, Maya Deren) The practice of associating particular deities to Catholic Saints constitutes an African slaves' legacy derived from the struggle to adapt African spiritual beliefs to those of the Christian religion, which European missionaries imposed on Native and Black captives during the colonization of the Americas.

We spend many years of our existence acquiring the lot of our collective belief system from our parents, guardians, siblings, educators, and other influential people. By the time we reach adulthood, we face the challenge to implement the concepts we learn throughout our infancy and development in age. Ultimately, we begin to experience the load of responsibility to perform independently, which eventually triggers feelings of doubt about our set of beliefs.

We progressively sense that our general understanding of the human existence does not provide us with a reliable explanation regarding our true objective on earth. Fortuitously, we find ourselves at the threshold of our personal belief system, where we face the choice to either accept the ideas from our collective belief system as the only guidelines for our behavior, or to step into the journey towards the acquisition of an infallible set of ideas that brings forth accurate interpretations of life events and fluctuations.

I

RECONCILIATION

The Caldron

The 50th Hexagram of the *I Ching*, the Chinese *Book of Changes*, speaks of the "Caldron." The Caldron is defined as a big cooking vessel made of bronze. Traditionally, it is used to cook food that will be offered to deities and angels. In order words, this huge pot holds purified nourishment given as sacrifice to the gods. Each human being possesses a "Caldron," or an inner vessel to consume impurities from offerings to divine entities.

The decision to claim a personal belief system enables the activation of our "Caldron." We should not carry our big and heavy "caldron" on our journeys to collect more integral additives for our belief system. We must take with us an empty and light container, which will better grasp the vivid ingredients that touch our senses.

The image of the Caldron's actuation translates that in our journey to acquire an enhanced meaning of life and of ourselves, we must come with humility, empty of arrogance and preconceived ideas. Duly, one day we will succeed in gathering the necessary elements or views to further the purifying of aliments in our "Caldron." This experience describes the course of Reconciliation or the path to Inner Peace, where we bring together various perspectives in the Holy Grail of transformation.

II

THE MATHEMATICS

1) The Tenth Department
2) Five Percent in the Tenth

The Tenth Department

After I left Ayiti in 1982 to enter the United States, like many immigrants I found myself in a foreign milieu, facing various kinds of limitation. I entered the country as a visitor and overstayed my visa. My parents' financial situation was deteriorating. I did not see what the future held in my own country. At the time, Duvalier son was the Ayisyen president. He and his wife wiped the State funds to profit their own group of people. They did not create any academic programs or job opportunities for the youth.

I became an illegal alien in the US. I spent about a year without any productive activities. I could not find any employment nor go to college. I stayed in Brooklyn, New York with one of my sisters and her family. Neither one of us held a green card. We were struggling financially. During the summer of that same year, a cousin of my mother (I will name him Uncle Henri for this book), a dean at East Stroudsburg University (East Stroudsburg State College, or ESSC, at the time), gave me the opportunity to enroll at the school in the Fall semester. He told me he always wanted to sponsor me, because he was informed of my excellent academic performance in grade school. I also believe that he wanted to repay my maternal grandmother for her compassion towards his family when they were facing financial hardship.

Despite my hope to take advantage of the prospect handed to me, the experience to attend ESSC did not aver itself to my big expectations. Uncle Henri and his wife were not hospitable hosts.

I was nineteen when I moved in with them in Pennsylvania. My handling of the English language required remedial instruction. The schedule of classes my mom's cousin set up for me was too advanced. He registered me for Music Appreciation, Psychology, College Algebra, and Spanish. I excelled in the latter considering my background in Latin etymology (a result of my schooling in Ayiti, a former Spanish and French colony). I was very devastated when I realized that I was failing the other subjects. As an international student, I knew I could perform better if the courses fit my high school background.

In addition to my unsuitable schedule of classes, my financial situation hindered my academic progress. I could not find employment on campus. Uncle Henri gave me a fifteen dollar bi-weekly allocation, or just a dollar fifty a day. Neither my parents nor my siblings residing in the US could send me any money, for they also were facing financial limitations at the time. I used to starve on campus. I could not focus in class for that matter. My uncle and I used to leave very early in the morning to reach the school punctually. I would start the day on an empty stomach, without any breakfast. My daily dollar-fifty allowance could only afford me a cup of coffee and a donut for the whole day. I would eat again at eight p.m. after we came back from the college and after dinner was finally served. I befriended a nice lady in the school cafeteria who agreed to sell to me on credit, but I could never catch up with my tab.

One day, I was so famished that I dared ask one of my relative's colleagues for some money to buy food on campus. Another time, I swallowed my pride and went to my uncle's office to tell him I was hungry. He gave me a few dollars and scolded me about spending my allowance unwisely. He surely did not approve that I sometimes would use my *bi-hebdomadal* $15 pittance to go to New York to visit my siblings and my boyfriend (whom I married later). I felt so isolated that some weekends I would just hop on a Greyhound bus to spend time with people I could really connect with. They would give me a few dollars to replace what I spent in bus and subway fares.

As time went by, I grew depressed at my uncle's house. In one instance, my hosts discussed the issue of AIDS (Acquired Immunodeficiency Syndrome) at the dinner table. They argued over the propaganda that Ayisyens were carriers of the AIDS virus. At one point, the college-educated African-American wife blurted out: "If the New York Times wrote it, then it's true!" Of course, my mom's cousin was furious while confronting his spouse's superciliousness. A state of deep mortification gripped my heart. I felt that no one could help me financially or emotionally. One night, I attempted suicide by swallowing some aspirin pills. The morning after, to my surprise I was still alive. I woke up, got ready, and went to school on an empty stomach as usual. I don't remember if I had my habitual coffee and donut, but I felt so sick that I went to see the campus nurse. I told her about my suicide attempt. I must have informed her that I had already thrown up my guts a few times during the day. She told me that I would be fine. She also recommended a visit to a psychologist at the college.

The day of my suicide attempt must have been a Friday. In the evening, my hosts decided to eat out at a Chinese restaurant. Despite the nauseous feeling on my chest and the heaviness in my head, I tried to eat as much as I could. I wished I could fill up my stomach more. It was the first time since I moved to Pennsylvania that I saw so much food. After we got back to the house, I felt sick. I began to throw up. I told my hosts I didn't feel well. I thought that I was going to die in a painful way. They looked at me with no concern in their eyes; the wife, a rictus on her lips. Today, I realize that they must have been thinking that I was pregnant.

Ignoring my depleted state of mind, I had to toughen up. I didn't die, but I felt like I hit a wall with nowhere to go. Deep inside of me I began to experience the feelings of failure. My collective belief system collapsed under the pressure of the challenges I was facing, including my inability to handle my schedule of classes, my financial hardship, and my hosts' inhospitality.

The following Monday I decided to pay a visit to the psychologist on campus. He was a middle-aged and bearded white man. He showed a kind disposition towards me. I remember that he inquired about the last dream I had before I decided to swallow the aspirin pills. I told him I saw someone shoot my father. The dream became the focus of our next session and the subsequent few we had... They helped me remember some suppressed memories about my relationship with my dad.

I didn't stay in Pennsylvania. I would have at least finished the semester. However, Uncle Henri unexpectedly proposed that it would be better for me to go back to Ayiti. He said he would sponsor me to re-enter the US legally. His suggestion seemed to be a long shot since the American Immigration and Naturalization Services would have penalized and prevented me from coming back for a few years after I overstayed my visa. One week, I took a trip to New York and never went back to my relative's house. I never returned to collect my personal belongings either. My uncle was upset about my decision. I had made up my mind that I didn't want to stay in Pennsylvania.

Somehow, I felt I would be more productive in New York. When I went back, I still faced financial hardship. However, I regained my liveliness. I enjoyed interacting with Ayisyens with whom I felt a strong cultural connection. I went to live with my sister who harbored me when I first came in the US. A few months later, I moved in with L., another of my sisters (two years older than me). That time of my life marks the beginning of my membership to the Ayisyen diaspora in New York.

Just like other immigrant groups, we Ayisyens have managed to graft our culture on a foreign land. We speak Creole among each other, but we taint it with various English words and expressions. For example, it is common to hear us say: "Mwen ap call ou pita" instead of "Mwen ap rele ou pita" (I will call you later). I, like many who still reside in Ayiti, used to think that my fellow brothers and sisters from the diaspora mix the languages to show off. Today, I can testify that most of us don't. This behavior is a characteristic of what former Ayisyen president, Jean Bertrand Aristide calls the "Tenth Department," a reference to the Ayisyen diaspora. Based on this denotation, all Ayisyen immigrants around the world make up an inclusive part of Ayiti, which comprised nine geographical departments. (In 2003, a tenth department was added to Ayiti's geographical map.)

Beside the language, we also maintain the Ayisyen diet, including plantain, fried pork (gryo), salted fish (moru), our famous squash soup (soup joumou), cooked usually on January first to celebrate our independence from France, rice and beans, mangoes, and other ethnic foods. To accommodate the community's various needs, many Ayisyens manage to acquire financial wealth and open businesses such as bakeries, restaurants, radio stations, newspapers, travel agencies, and other types of commercial places. Away from the natal land, the Tenth has also kept the religious traditions alive. Its members not only attend Christian services, they also become active and integral church participants. They have succeeded in securing the performance of masses in Creole. Some Christian groups such as the Baptist and the Pentecostal have set up their respective churches in areas like Brooklyn, New York with a dense Ayisyen population.

One aspect of the Tenth Department is that it encompasses Ayisyens from all regions and all social backgrounds of Ayiti itself. This feature sets up the ground for a new experience as people from all cardinal points of the country coexist in foreign lands. Often times, the table is turned, especially in America, the land of opportunities where any individual can work very hard to become prosperous or hit the jackpot overnight to claim millions of dollars. Therefore, an Ayisyen from a poor family may ascend financially in the US, and a person from a privileged upbringing can really struggle to make ends meet.

Additionally, the phenomenon of people from the South, North, East, and West of a country revealing to each other new facets of their mutual culture in the context of a foreign land, stretches the boundaries of the migrators' collective belief system. One key example of this issue is the importance of Voodoo as a way of life among Ayisyens. Many people in the world, including some Ayisyens, learn of Voodoo in a pejorative depiction. For example, when I was growing up in Ayiti, I used to hear stories about loup-garous (werewolves) flying to collect people's souls. I thought that was Voodoo, and I feared it. One definition that the Webster's dictionary provides is "a person who deals with spells and necromancy." Today, I dare to defer, and insist on shedding some light on the meaning of Voodoo.

After I became a member of the Tenth Department in Brooklyn, New York with its version of collective views and its spiritual vibrations in relation to the Voodoo tradition, I came to the understanding that Voodoo is the Tao, or The Way that the Chinese philosopher, Lao-

Tzu teaches about. Voodoo, like any spiritual path, reinforces the awareness that we are essentially energy, and as such, we must live our lives. Therefore, the Voodooist perspective reminds us constantly about the intentions of the heart or the emotions behind the choices we make as individual bundles of energy. A person whose heart is filled with hatred, violence, or envy will affect her environment in a destructive way. On the other hand, when our heart contains love, empathy, or kindness, we emit constructive vibrations around us and towards all living beings.

The Voodooist view stresses people's essence in energy. It involves devotional rituals with the power of our intentions. When we reach this state of detachment from physical limitations, we are faced with choices that challenge the heart to follow the path of unity, courage, love, fairness, and truth, or stay on the trail of discord, frailty, wickedness, and deceit. People make their individual choices. Voodoo is spiritual knowledge that deeply permeates the Ayisyen belief system. It emphasizes the human essence in energy, and underlines the intentions of the heart. Therefore, anyone involved in the manipulation of energy will affect the environment according to the content of her or his heart. Essentially, Voodoo is a path that tests the heart.

In the Tenth Department, I met fellow country women and men from all four corners of Ayiti. I learned about the regional and class divisions among us, which affect our sentiments for each other. In turn, despite our patriotic solidarity and our collective system of beliefs, our interactions with each other remain fragmented by erroneous social constructs. Amid such complex cultural make-up, I felt at home. I regained a feeling of aspiration, in spite of my humbling status of undocumented alien. During that time, I strived to be productive. I could not pursue a college education yet. However, I found employment "under the table." I did not pay taxes on my wages. I did not earn a lot. But on one occasion, I managed to send a little bit of money to my parents. I felt so proud of myself.

One day, my sister L. and her boyfriend introduced the idea of liberation among our group of acquaintances. Their view involved freedom from the system of social norms that dictate people's patterns of behavior. One main example of these models consists on the notion that we must work for somebody else to earn a living. Our main goal transpired the vision to become industrious and self-sufficient by finding ways to generate financial resources for our daily survival.

I was twenty at the time the idea of liberation sprouted within our group, including my boyfriend. Personally, I found the thought appealing. Many of us quit our jobs, and began living according to the philosophy of rejecting established social standards. We brainstormed about creative ways to become productive: starting a newsletter concerning community issues, organizing cultural events, opening an office to offer multiple services, among other objectives that appealed to our fancy. We did manage to organize a successful social event one weekend. We also obtained an interview with Dadou Pasquet, the very talented guitarist and maestro of the Ayisyen Magnum Band. Unfortunately, our lack of capital and collateral posed a major impediment to our ideal of liberation. Most of us had no choice but to look for employment to earn our daily bread. Nevertheless, the seed of mental emancipation from the system opened our brains to new conceptualizations of the human experience on earth. Incidentally, we became exposed to the Five Percenters' philosophy when we met Born Allah, an Ayisyen neighbor of my sister's boyfriend. We called him "Born" or "Allah." This encounter conveys the dynamic fusion of thoughts in the Tenth.

Five Percent in the Tenth

Born gave us an electrifying jolt with the statement: "The Black man is God." We listened with avid interest when he revealed to us the Five Percenters' teachings, which central claim is that eighty-five percent of the world population is blind, deaf, and dumb about their true historical origin. Ten percent is informed about the truth, but conspires to keep it a secret. The Five Percenters are people who know their history and strive to implement its legacy of principles in their lives. They reject the Ten Percent's social guidelines for obedient citizenry and advocate righteousness instead.

The basic premise of Five Percenters helped me recognize a major flaw in the Ayisyen collective belief system. When I was a child, I often silently wondered why Jesus, the Virgin Mary, and most Catholic Saints were depicted as White people. I still felt a lot of pride about the fact that Ayiti is the first Black Republic of modern history. However, I couldn't fight off this sentiment of inferiority vis-à-vis White people in general. Consequently, hearing for the first time the association of the Divine with the Black race caught my full attention. I really wanted to hear more about the Five Percenters' standpoint.

Historically, Clarence 13X, a former member of the Nation of Islam, began the Five Percenters' movement in 1964. He taught his followers that no mystery God exists, and that the Black man is God. Clarence 13X renamed himself Allah. According to his views, the Black woman corresponds symbolically to the earth as well as the moon, or a reflection of the Black man viewed as the sun itself. Hence, he formally identified the group as "The Nation of Gods and Earths." Today, much data is available on 13X and its legacy.

Just like my sister, her boyfriend, and some of our friends, I began reading about the Five Percenters' philosophy, and adopting their prescriptions for a righteous way of life. I eliminated certain items from my diet, such as meat (except for fish), white sugar, sweetened beverages, and all processed foods as much as possible. I stopped using relaxing agents in my hair and wore clothing that covered three-fourth of my body just like the earth is seventy-five percent covered with water. Additionally, "The Supreme Mathematics," a philosophical tool that Clarence 13X devised for his followers, became a daily guide in my life.

The idea behind the "Supreme Mathematics" is to "add" or "build." Each number, and to that effect, each date of the month corresponds to a principle that Five Percenters strive to implement accordingly. When they meet, Gods and Earths remind each other of the "Mathematics" of the day and they proceed to build on it in their conversations. For example, on the first of the month they build on "Knowledge" corresponding to the number 1. On the second of the month, they discuss "Wisdom" associated with the number 2, and so on. In the case of a two-digit number such as 13, 1 (Knowledge) is added to 3 (Understanding), equaling 4 (Culture or Freedom). The Supreme Mathematics enable us to avoid idle talks and engage in constructive exchanges and actions. This philosophical tool constitutes a code of conduct that redirects Five Percenters' focus to a righteous and sophisticated level of perception.

Clarence 13X also uses the Supreme Alphabet as a reinforcing guide to the Mathematics. He created this system of philosophical principles by linking each letter of the alphabet to ideas that stress positive thinking as well as cultural awareness according to Five Percenters' standards. For example, the letter "p" stands for power, which conveys truth. The letter "s" stands for self or savior, which translates into the notion that people acquire knowledge to save themselves first before trying to save others. Interestingly, the letter "x" means "unknown," clarifying the reason that Five

Percenters and members of The Nation of Islam adopt the letter "x" as their last name. This choice corresponds to the rejection of last names such as "Johnson" or "Jackson" that constantly remind Black people of slavery times when our ancestors were imposed slave masters' names.

Besides the Supreme Mathematics and Alphabet, 13Xs teachings include 120 lessons or degrees consisting of questions and answers that Gods and Earths aim to memorize. The Degrees constitute elements of "building" interactions as well as behavior molding. First and foremost, they identify who the Devil is and who's God. Five Percenters learn that the Devil is the White man, or the weak and wicked person who uses trick knowledge to deceive other people. The lesson that I believe makes up a pungent revelation to black people in search of their true identity is: "The Black man is God." Incidentally, the Degrees teach that the mystery God which Christianity and Islam lead their members to worship does not exist. This teaching erased the mystification about the Divine for my sister, her boyfriend, some of our friends, and me. We freely decided to learn more about 13Xs views.

From the Degrees, Five Percenters study that "Word is bond." This statement means: "Speak the truth." Another lesson teaches: "Take everything from knowledge to born." As mentioned earlier, the number 1 translates into Knowledge. Born corresponds to the number 9. Therefore, just like it takes women nine months to carry a baby to full term, in everything we say and do, we must remember to start from the beginning. Then, we will succeed by proceeding in stages. Earths and Gods attend monthly meetings, or "Universal Parliaments" to engage in building sessions as well as further their education about the group's philosophy. They also discuss other organizational issues and concerns.

At first, the choice we made to be liberated fascinated people around us. We had an ideal to use our creativity to become productive in innovative ways. However, the Five Percenters' way of life within the Tenth Department demanded a higher leap against social norms. It involved the rejection of old beliefs and the courage to be different with the application of radical principles of behavior.

Not eating pork meat for example constitutes a big shock for many Ayisyens who view fried pork (gryo) as an integral recipe of their ethnic cuisine. Additionally, keeping our hair free of relaxers and wearing African clothing (women, bodies three-fourths covered) defied the aesthetic standards of both the Ayisyen community and the Western society.

Furthermore, our acceptance of Clarence 13Xs standpoint that the Black man is God created fear in people who've all their lives accepted the existence of a White God sitting in heaven. Adopting Islamic names also represented a drastic step towards our transformation.[2] Our new behavior grew into a big challenge to the collective belief system of the Ayisyen community. People around us became critical about our choices and began to distance themselves from us. We were faced with the hard realization that we needed to find ways to provide at least food, clothes, and shelter to ourselves and our children (a basic of the Five Percenters' premise, which teaches Gods and Earths to be economically self-sustaining, and keep from applying for Government subsidies).

The decision to become liberated and financially self-sufficient coupled with the choice of living according to the Supreme Mathematics and Alphabet resulted in beneficial effects, especially in reviving our cultural identity. On the other hand, it brought about material challenges. The attempt to create independent means of survival requires start-up monetary funds, which we as well as our group of friends were lacking. The cost of life in New York was increasing. The pricing rate of rent especially was skyrocketing. Our financial stagnation became extremely burdensome. At times, we could not even feed ourselves.

On an individual level, the system of beliefs I held most of my life was crumbling under both the Liberation and Mathematics

---

[2] This choice reflects the background of the founder of the Nation of Gods and Earths. Indeed, 13X was a former member of The Nation of Islam (NOI). According to some reports, he left the organization in 1963, because his categorical teaching regarding God's identity diverged from the NOI's doctrine. Nonetheless, his philosophy sprang from his past association with the group.

standpoints. I had reached the threshold of my personal belief system. After I came back from Pennsylvania, within a year my boyfriend and I had a child. He quit his job after we embraced the idea of liberation. Two years later, we had another baby. Our economic challenges became a strain on our intimate relationship. We couldn't even afford to rent an apartment.

One day, I decided to move to New Jersey with my other sister who housed me when I first came in the US. After a few months, my boyfriend joined my children and me in Trenton, New Jersey. Not long after, we got married. Since he's a naturalized American citizen, I became eligible for legal residency in the United States. At first, I was granted working papers. I immediately applied for employment where my sister and her husband worked. When I finally obtained my green card, I applied for educational grants and other governmental subsidies for low-income families.

In New Jersey, my husband and I managed to acquire financial stability. The cost of life was more reasonable in comparison to that of New York. After we found employment, in no time we managed to move in our own apartment. During that time, we applied ourselves to maintain the Five Percenters' way of life. We had already changed our first names and those of our children. Some people thought we were Muslim. We felt isolated. My sister's oldest son was open to 13Xs teachings. Nonetheless, we couldn't find any other Ayisyen of like mind in the New Jerseyan Tenth.

The challenge to locate a vibrant Five Percenters population around us did not stop our commitment to live righteously. Based on this resolve, we decided to home school our children. I stayed home with our son and daughter. I also looked for Afrocentric activities and programs for young children in the New Jersey area. My search was rewarded when I found the Timbuktu Academy, a preschool which a Muslim couple funded in the heart of Trenton. We enrolled our children, who received an Afrocentric academic foundation from their teachers. We also learned about Black history, and celebrated African American holidays such as Kwanzaa. The Timbuktu Academy staff gave us a lead to another Afrocentric institution, the Afrikan People's Action School. There, our children were able to move on to higher grades and further their Black oriented education. We did our best to stay above water by ensuring that our babies acquired the awareness of their cultural roots at a young age.

PEACE

III

ANOTHER REALITY

A Native's Spiritual Narrative

My years of studies and implementation of the Five Percenters' philosophy make up a time of mental purification, when I cleared my head of fallacious ideas from my collective belief system. I used to accept the notion that White people are smarter than Black people. I used to think that straight or curly hair is more beautiful than coarse hair. I used to feed into the images shown on TV about the White male hero, the depiction of Native Americans and Africans as savages and other subjective pictures feeding the mental image that the White race is superior to all other races. I grew up reading romantic novels that described feelings, which triggered and reinforced fantasies about romantic relationships alien to my true origin and reality. I used to envision God as a White man, even when he came to save me in my childhood nightmares. I used to live well in exile of my cultural identity.

Unknown to my physical eyes, after I moved to New Jersey, I brought back to my "Caldron" the content of the vessel that captured Clarence 13Xs teachings to his followers. I learned most importantly I too am born in God's image. I learned to live righteously according to the Supreme Mathematics. I learned to appreciate Black beauty and Black history. I also learned that Knowledge is infinite, which opened my eyes to new world views.

Incidentally, one day, my younger brother (a Massachusetts resident) came for a visit in New Jersey. He told my husband and me about Carlos Castaneda's books. My brother lived in New York for a short while. He was also exposed to the Five Percenters' philosophy. We could still carry building conversations; hence, his suggestion that "we do the knowledge" about the author's work. He warned us, however, that the acquaintance who first introduced him to Castaneda's books believed the content of his books reflects the writer's experiences with hallucinogenic drugs. My sibling left us a copy of *A Yaqui Way of Knowledge*.

The quote on the back cover of Castaneda's first book provoked an ineffable feeling of curiosity within me. It reads:

> For me there is only the travelling on paths that have heart, on any path that may have heart. There I travel, and the only worthwhile challenge is to travel its full length. And there I travel, looking, looking Breathlessly. (Don Juan)

Both my husband and I delved into the author's books. I was and I still am fascinated with the philosophical views the author shares in his work. The readings of Castaneda's books marked the beginning of a new search to collect more ingredients for my "Caldron."

Carlos Castaneda's books relate his apprenticeship under an old Native American named Don Juan, whom he met in Arizona. During the time he was a student at the University of California, the author began an investigative journey in the Southwest of the US to collect information about the usage of medicinal herbs among Natives. The outcome of his inquiry unexpectedly unraveled cultural practices as well as philosophical concepts that provide a stunning and valid meaning to human life in the universe.

Castaneda was particularly inquisitive about peyote, a cactus that grows in the Southwest of the United States and in Mexico. The button of this plant contains mescaline, a hallucinogenic drug. Don Juan, a native of Sonora, Mexico, agreed to teach the author about the properties of the cactus and other plants only if he (Castaneda) became his apprentice. Indeed, the old Yaqui was a sorcerer. According to his system of beliefs, he "saw" an omen, which indicated Castaneda as the chosen man to whom he would teach his mystical connaissance as well as the cultural practices from his lineage of spiritual leaders.

The old Yaqui was the head, or "nagual" of a group of sorcerers. He defined his title as a level of mastery in his knowledge of "sorcery" that allows him to be a teacher or a guide for people who possess natural ability to become sorcerers. Don Juan himself had a teacher or a "benefactor" who chose him as the next nagual who would continue the tradition of the line of sorcerers, or "seers" who can perceive covert aspects of life to the physical eyes.

The nagual did not simply acquiesce to take the scholar as a student. He gave him challenges to overcome with the simple goal for the latter to find in his heart the real purpose behind his desire to learn about specific plants. The first test consisted in the task for the author to find on the old man's porch the most auspicious spot or a place where he could experience a personal feeling of inner security. Castaneda actually found two spots that produced particular inner sensations as he rolled his body on the ground. The first point created a feeling of anxiety inside of him. He experienced a surge of well-being when he reached the second. He tried to go back to the first spot, but retracted with apprehension. He went back to the other place and fell asleep after a few minutes. When he woke up, Don Juan told him that he had solved the first riddle. He added that everybody should be aware of their beneficial as well as their enemy spot. This is especially true for people who are seeking knowledge in abstract reality.

After the nagual accepted Castaneda as his apprentice, he had him experience respective states of non-ordinary reality with the ingestion of peyote as well as jimson-weed and the smoke inhalation of a type of mushrooms. Effectively, in the introduction of *The Teachings of Don Juan: A Yaqui Way of Knowledge*, Castaneda wrote:

> Since before Europeans, American Indians have known the hallucinogenic properties of these three plants. Because of their properties, the plants have been widely employed for pleasure, for curing, for witchcraft, and for attaining a state of ecstasy.

Don Juan explained to his new student that the last two plants he listed are used to beckon power or an "ally." He defined "ally" as a power that an individual can attract for assistance, support and enlightenment through any life endeavor. He also stated that peyote makes up the seat of Mescalito, a spirit who entrusts to potential adherents, wisdom, or the right way to live.

Don Juan became strongly convinced that the author was the one to whom he would have to teach the secret mastery of his knowledge after the latter ingested peyote for the first time. In that instance, Mescalito danced with Castaneda. According to the old Native American, that event constituted a powerful and undeniable omen, which pointed the writer as the chosen apprentice who would lead the new circle of sorcerers in Don Juan's lineage.

As required by his tradition, before the old Yaqui revealed the secrets of his knowledge to his student, he carefully stated:

> A man of knowledge goes to war wide-awake, with fear, with respect, and with absolute assurance. Going to knowledge or going to war in any other manner is a mistake, and whoever makes it will live to regret his steps. (*The Teachings of Don Juan*, p.23)

Under Don Juan's tutelage, Castaneda learned about the powers in the Jimson weed and a mixture of mushrooms, which the nagual referred to respectively as "the devil's weed" and "the little smoke." Each part of the devil's weed has a special property, but its power rests in the roots. The author describes the experience of becoming a bird, and learning how to fly after internal and topical absorptions of mixtures from the roots of the plant. The nagual proceeded to teach his apprentice about the systematic collection of the little mushrooms and the other ingredients that are used in the meticulous preparation of the "little smoke." Castaneda wrote about the first time he inhaled the vapor from the dry mixture. He felt like he didn't have a physical body anymore, and he could sink into a wall.

Some readers argue that Don Juan is a fictional character out of Carlos Castaneda's hallucinogenic dreams from experimenting with drugs. They dismiss the veracity of his field reports. Others such as my brother, my husband, and I are really fascinated with the author's vivid descriptions about another reality. For us, it is not unusual to hear stories about people transforming themselves into birds. Both Don Juan's and the Voodooist premises understand people as vessels of energy. Therefore, both paths involve the handling of energy and deeply reflect the intentions of the heart. (Interestingly, the Catholic religion depicts some saints such as Sacred Heart of Jesus pointing at their heart.) Importantly enough, the old Yaqui told his student that "seers" in ancient times mastered the ability to handle people's awareness.

My fascination for Castaneda's work grew in intensity after the following experience on a New York subway train. At that time, I was reading the author's books with great avidity. I remember sitting on the train, my mind full of Don Juan's lessons to his student. Suddenly, I heard a voice close to my right ear. It was a woman's voice. I turned my head, and saw two strange grayish eyes. She told me to look at the Mexicans sitting across from us. Then, she asked if I've ever noticed how different they look from the other Hispanics. I was polite and smiled. I didn't know what to say. The train stopped and she left. I knew that this meeting was part of the unordinary reality I was reading about. Therefore, I kept at it breathlessly.

Castaneda is the author of many books, including *A Separate Reality*, *Tales of Power*, *Fire from Within*, and *The Power of Silence*, which provide intense descriptions regarding his supernatural experiences under Don Juan's wise guidance. The central premise of the Yaqui's teachings is for us human beings to fight our greatest enemy, self-importance. This prescription is very significant for people who possess the knowledge of energy manipulation. Incidentally, in *Fire from Within*, the author relates a conversation he had with the nagual. Don Juan told his apprentice that self-importance is at the center of what is righteous and what is corrupted inside of us. A "warrior" strives to overcome the latter strategically. The old Native American uses the expression "man of knowledge" as well as "warrior" to refer to people like himself who are in quest of a more stupendous meaning of life than that of a series of materialistic experiences easily described in logical expressions.

We, as human beings, tend most often to feel offended by other living beings' actions. This type of feelings drains our energy. Once a "man of knowledge" succeeds in battling self-importance, she or he can rechannel the unused energy towards constructive goals such as healing and performing miraculous deeds. Don Juan revealed to

Castaneda that warriors who lived at the time Spaniards invaded the Americas began a new breed of sorcerers. Those women and men identified five attributes that reside within a warrior's heart, and enable them to counter off their self-importance: control, discipline, forbearance, timing, and will. However, they also detected an external agent that challenges a warrior's bid for detachment in facing self-importance stimuli. This outside agent is referred to as "petty tyrant."

Don Juan defines a petty tyrant as a tormentor, or someone who either holds the power of life and death over warriors, or annoys them to distraction. He also provides a list of various kinds of petty tyrants such as "small fry petty tyrants" who exasperate and bother a person tirelessly. The Native man of knowledge even contends that a warrior who meets a petty tyrant is very fortunate, since this special agent is the most important attribute in the fight against self-importance. Don Juan evokes the historical fact that the new breed of sorcerers from his tradition emerged during the European colonization of the Americas. The new hostile settlers represented petty tyrants who gave warriors a sure opportunity to fight off self-importance:

> We know that nothing can tamper the spirit of a warrior as much as the challenge of dealing with impossible people in positions of power. Only under those conditions can warriors acquire the sobriety and serenity to stand the power of the unknowable.
> (Don Juan, *Fire from Within*, p. 19)

Castaneda's report about his apprenticeship and his conversations with Don Juan can help a person acquire an expanded scope on life meaning. According to the Yaqui seer, the purpose of the new group of sorcerers is to convince their students of the untapped natural human abilities. The discussions about the "assemblage point" in most of Castaneda's books provide a sheer light on the subject.

Don Juan revealed to his student that people learn to assemble their perception of the world from other individuals around them. Then, they constantly remind themselves about their learned reality. Otherwise, human beings would develop odd behavior patterns in

RECONCILIATION

the eyes of their fellow community members. The nagual added that we can "see" other layers of life possibilities when the assemblage point shifts. Sorcerers develop the ability to move other people's assemblage point and can teach their students the skill to perform such a magical act.

As I read Carlos Castaneda's books, I understood that I may never become a sorcerer's apprentice, nor experience states of non-ordinary reality with the consumption of peyote and other hallucinogenic plants. I may not mature into a woman of knowledge nor interact with allies in this lifetime either. However, I grew more and more fascinated with Don Juan's wise teachings, and strove to implement them in my daily life. I began to fight my lousy self-importance and to develop an expanded view concerning the human existence on earth.

IV

THE AUSARIAN EXPERIENCE

Finding the Tree of Life

1) The Neteru
2) The Story of Ausar
3) A Path with a Heart

The Neteru

By the time I finished reading Carlos Castaneda's books, my Ayisyen collective belief system was in ramble. The platform of my fundamental views on life was collapsing under the impact of events around me and my interactions with other people. I had just found the root of my Black origin that in no time a deeper understanding of the human existence on earth opened itself to me with Don Juan's teachings. I was on my knees pushing upward to persevere in the daily application of the Five Percenters' standpoint and a Native American's perspective on life.

Adopting new ways of being and acting, especially claiming a Black origin in this world, and trying to fight self-importance simultaneously, render a person an oddity in other people's eyes (oftentimes of familiar faces). Nonetheless, I persisted in the journey of claiming my personal belief system.

The Five Percenters' views are undoubtedly impregnated with a considerable degree of self-importance (the righteous kind, to quote Don Juan). Claiming my Black identity in terms of my physical appearance, visualizing that I, too, was created in God's image, as well as reinforcing the daily philosophical concepts of the NGE provokes a feeling of self-worth and self-pride regarding the White race's domination, the Ten Percent's oppression, and the Eighty-Five Percent's ignorance. All Black people must be exposed to an effective reminder of their true origin. I'm extremely grateful that I did have such opportunity by learning 13Xs legacy. When human beings are in touch with their historical past as well as their ancestral lineage, they are more anchored in their self-worth and more able to grow stronger culturally. Incidentally, the Jamaican forerunner, Marcus Garvey wrote:

> A people without knowledge of their history, origin, and culture is like a tree without roots.

After I poured in the "Caldron" the concepts I learned through reading Carlos Castaneda's books, I involved myself with the challenge to claim my Black identity on one hand and to fight self-importance (that compelling egocentrism) on the other. From that inner strife, I grew more and more estranged to my environment. I employed a lot of energy to try maintaining quietude within and without; to no avail. My relationship with people around me became superfluous. No one could relate to the new habits and attitude I was adopting. Even my relationship with my husband was deteriorating. His various extra-marital interactions with other women constituted the challenge of a petty tyrant in my life. Everybody could see the wind blow through my heart.

The only strong and healthy relationship during that stage of my life was with my children. By then my husband and I had a third child together. We gave him an African name. I ensured that my sons and daughter learn about Black history and their culture. They were very receptive. We spent much quality time together. They were a great source of joy for me. Somehow, I knew I would be alright. Perhaps the mixture in the "Caldron" had begun an imperceptible process of consummation to seal the first blocks to the foundation of my personal belief system.

One day, my sister, L., my husband, and one of our children's teachers began discussing about an Afrocentric group that held workshops on holistic practices like meditation, healthy diet, and Yoga. They expressed a profound fascination apropos the teachings of the Ausar Auset Society, headquartered in New York City at the time. My sister bought some audio tapes of workshops on cosmology and introduction to meditation facilitated by Ra Un Nefer Amen, the organization's founder. The discourse concerning the Tree of Life and the different types of men captured my interest. I decided to learn more about the views and the practices of the Afrocentric group.

Ra Un Nefer Amen, also known as Shekem Ur Shekem, and a group of priests from his spiritual tradition established the Ausar Auset Society in 1973 with an emphasis on the true origin of Black people. Their vision was to institute an environment where individuals of African descent can gather as a community to reconnect with their cultural and spiritual past. They also developed classes relating to holistic living, including instruction on healthy diet as well as stress management practices. Through various weekly workshops, Shekem Ur Shekem and his acolytes teach members and other participants about the philosophy of ancient African cultures, particularly that of ancient Egypt or Kamit. Furthermore, students are introduced to systems of divination such as the Metu Neter system of oracle as tools for spiritual development. This training is complemented with Yoga instructions, breathing techniques, and other forms of life force cultivation. Over the years, the Ausar Auset Society has expanded itself to establish locations in cities like Atlanta, Georgia and Philadelphia, Pennsylvania as well as in other countries such as France and Trinidad.

Ra Un Nefer Amen is the author of many books including a few volumes of *Metu Neter, Healing the Errors of Living and Afrocentric Guide to a Spiritual Union.* The *Metu Neter Vol. I*, which is accompanied with a deck of cards for the Metu Neter Oracle System, encompasses the spiritual leader integral perspective on spirituality with an emphasis on ancient Egyptian culture.

In the introduction, Amen provides a discourse concerning knowledge of self in terms of voluntary and involuntary behavior. He states that:

> ...dualization of our being into two fundamental sets of function is the central theme of self-knowledge. (*Metu Neter, Vol. I*, p. 5)

He proceeds to explain that one aspect of ourselves is in charge of activities that we control, such as driving or walking. Another side of ourselves rules over activities which we don't direct including hunger, thirst, or learning new words.

The author of the *Metu Neter* uses his introductory remarks on the subject of human behavior to suggest that in the physical world, there exist three kinds of people: the first depends more on voluntary actions for survival and productivity; the second on involuntary performances, which are in harmony with the intuitive or the all-knowing part of ourselves; the third on the balance between the first two behaviors. According to Ra Un Nefer Amen, Kamit's flourishing era is attributed to its people's reliance on the latter (behavior). He cites additional ancient civilizations such as Kush (Ethiopia), Indus Kush (Black India), and Canaan as pioneers to great achievements. He writes:

> Because of their people's ability to learn from the internal part of their being, with its Storehouse of knowledge concerning every secret of the world, they were able to intuit 6000+ years ago, the knowledge that forms the basis of our civilization (religion, mathematics, metallurgy, government, architecture, painting sculpturing, algebra, science, etc.). (*Metu Neter, Vol. I*, pp 7, 8)

Amen's investigative chapters on the subject of Black civilizations, their achievements as well as their way of life, provide various references from scholars who confer the origin of civilization to people of African descent. For example, the renowned Greek historian Herodotus reported from his travel that the Egyptian of Kamit had Black skin and wooly hair. Pierre Montet and his *Eternal Egypt*, Jacqueta Hawkes and her *First Great Civilizations*, Rama Shankar Tripathi and his *History of Ancient India*, constitute additional sources to Amen's work. One important aspect of the *Metu Neter Vol I* is the reviving discussions about the beliefs and practices that characterize ancient cultures like Kamit. The people from those civilizations understood there must be a scheme to human existence on earth. They devoted special time to find the intuition to such a blueprint and encountered a variety of electromagnetic forces, which they managed to map as the Tree of Life.

While mapping the forces governing human behavior, African people understood that these various manifestations of energy represent natural laws ruling over all aspects and events of life. Ra Un Nefer Amen established the Ausar Auset Society to provide its members

Reconciliation

with the opportunity to study cosmogony and to reclaim a way of life that follows the concept of the Paut Neteru. This involves self-introspection through meditating and chanting mantra to stimulate the activation of the spheres on the Tree.

THE PAUT NETERU (TREE OF LIFE)

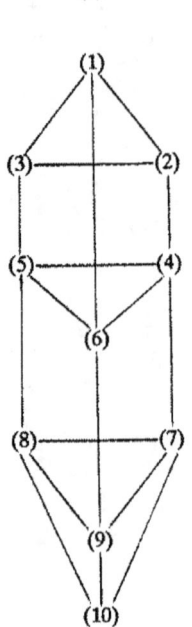

(Metu Neter Vol. I, p. 64)

The "0" above the Tree represents the essence of all life as energy and matter. The "10" at the bottom of the Tree corresponds to the physical world matter molded in the different aspects and forms of life. The nine spheres of the Tree of Life or the Paut Neteru displays people's spiritual make-up or the differentiation within ourselves into interconnected and complementary clusters. About the Paut Neteru, Amen writes:

"They are what the Kamitians called the Neteru, the Yorubas call the Orishas, and Westerners have translated as deities, Archangels, angels, etc."

The first sphere on the Tree corresponds to our true self, or the faculty we must ultimately awaken to stop identifying with the material aspect of life and reclaim our essence in Amen. There resides the deity

Ausar as the omnipresent expression of peace in the physical world. Of a person who succeeds in achieving the Ausar state, Shekem Ur Shekem writes:

> He will be totally free of the control of likes, dislikes, love, hatred, fear, anger, and the whole of emotions and desires.

The discourse on the first sphere of the Tree reminded me about Don Juan's quote regarding a path with a heart and the warrior's battle against self-importance. I decided to embrace the Ausarian view breathlessly and to traverse its full length.

The second sphere of the Tree of Life houses the deity Tehuti. Herein dwells the all-knowing or omniscient aspect of our essential nature. Just like the Five Percenters' philosophy, the second sphere corresponds to wisdom, our ability to intuit and speak the truth. When we still our thought process to cease the constant shutter in our mind, we achieve clarity or a state of unbiased certainty within. Sages are people who have perfected the cultivation of this immanent faculty.

The third sphere of the Paut Neteru houses the deity Seker (Sekert for the female aspect), reflecting the omnipotence of our true nature. We can manifest the all-powerful attribute of our spiritual make-up through the activation of the third sphere. The awakening of this ability requires great discipline to chant, pray, or perform the rites that will affect the physical world. Ausar, Tehuti, and Seker(t) constitute the three highest faculties on the Tree. Only people who devote their life to spiritual cultivation succeed to tap into the unlimited probability at humanity's reach. They manifest leadership qualities to teach and perform feats for the betterment of humanity. Clarence 13X, Don Juan, and Ra Un Nefer Amen are examples of such individuals.

Maat is the most contiguous deity to the first pyramid on the Paut Neteru. Sitting on the fourth sphere, she is depicted as a female manifestation of our spirit. Holding a scale weighing a heart against a feather, she reminds us to keep a light heart in every situation. In the Kamitian tradition, she represents the Goddess of law and order. She is also the female counterpart of Tehuti, and as such, symbolizes Truth and Purity. Maat corresponds to the highest manifestation of Love: giving to others without any expectation of repayment or gratification. Students of the Ausar Auset Society learn the meditation *Men Ab Em Aungk Em Maat* (Keeping the Heart Stable to Live Truth) to ignore negative emotions that cause them to be easily offended by other people's actions and misdeeds. Thus, they can generate feelings of kindness inside. The meditation on the Maat sphere reminded me a great deal of Don Juan's teachings about the warrior's ultimate challenge to combat self-importance. It reinforced my commitment to complete the full length of my association with the Ausar Auset Society.

Appropriately, the faculty to fight for law and order resides in the second pyramid of the Paut Neteru next to the deity Maat. Herukhuti stands in the mathematical center of the Tree as our sense of Justice. Fire is the element associated with this sphere. Indeed, the fight for Truth and Justice requires passion and determination. True to Don Juan's lessons, the warrior is at war with her own self-importance. Hence, Herukhuti is willing to cut off her head for law and order.

The sixth sphere, Heru constitutes the diagrammatical center of the Tree of Life. "It is the faculty where the equilibrium of Man's being is established." (*Metu Neter I*, p. 9) Heru represents our ability to grow spiritually by observing Maat's principles of Divine Law. Effectively, spheres six and four add up to Ten, as all complementary spheres of the Tree do. The Ausarian perspective evokes the Men Am Em Aungk Em Maat as Heru's eternal goal to succeed in the struggle against his enemies in anger, envy, greed, lust, covertness… This center also houses the fire element, since we employ our will to change ourselves and choose the path of Truth. Both the Herukhuti and Heru faculties require our concerns in adopting habits that conserve our energy so that we can manifest constructive behavior in our environment. This second pyramid of our spiritual make-up encompasses our commitment and courage to choose the Truth.

In the Kamitic tradition, the energy within the seventh sphere of the Tree, Het Heru is translated as the house of Heru. In Voodoo she's Freda, the Goddess of beauty, harmony, and sweetness. She symbolizes the energy of fertility, which invokes our creative faculty. Before we experience the drive to change and transcend erroneous beliefs and wrong habits, we first visualize the behavior or the goal we aspire to achieve. She's the house of joy and pleasure where our passion for Truth is revived. Freda is impregnated with the embryo of our will. The cultivation of this faculty relates to the safeguard of the life force within, our sexual energy, and the seed of change. The discussion about Het Heru reminds us of the Five Percenters' prescriptions to apply the Mathematics in building conversations and interactions.

The eighth sphere houses Sebek, our ability to process information and to segregate. Therein dwells the voice of reason. Sebek (Legba for the Voodooist) allows us to acquire our belief system: the lot of who we believe we are and what we believe is right. This faculty is critical in our ability to validate accurately and constantly our membership to our physical environment. Nonetheless, when we only use this part of our spirit to interpret life events, we fail to see the interdependence that characterizes their occurrence in time and space. Legba also governs our ability to verbally express the ideas we acquire from all sources. Evidently, the energy in the eighth sphere corresponds to our belief system: collective and personal. The former usually teaches us to be reasonable and social beings, and in many instances, fails to show us the way to tap into higher spiritual potentials. When we acknowledge the flaws in our collective belief system, we've reached the threshold of our personal belief system where we search for new views that will auspiciously change our interpretation of the human objective on earth.

Auset, the faculty within the ninth sphere of The Paut Neteru, constitutes the seat of our identity in the world, where we learn what to think and how to behave. She is associated with our ability to nurture, to follow, and to remember. She's the symbol of motherhood. The memories of our past experiences, including traumatic ones reflected in our behavior patterns, are linked to this innate ability. We invoke Auset in regressive meditations to recollect past emotional disturbances resulting to an inner storage of hellish and sick feelings that dictate our reactions in interactions with the outer world. As the counterpart of the first sphere, Ausar, she's a warrior. Her devotion to reject wrong beliefs and cultivate constructive behavior must be infallible. She's also fierce as a vulture in her protection of her Children.*[3] In the Voodoo tradition, Auset compares to Ezuli Danto, a Black Goddess holding a child on her arm. She has two noticeable scratch marks on her cheeks, which according to some symbolize her untiring fight for her children's life.

The tenth sphere at the base of the Tree houses matter in its differentiated forms, animated by vital sensations. This is the physical body, subject to various feelings such as hunger, thirst, love, anger, joy, sadness…and moved by external stimuli like sounds and smells. This sphere, also known as the Khaibit in the Kamitic tradition, corresponds to the animal part of our lot as human beings. Most people allow the vibrations from the Khaibit to control the faculties housed in the adjacent pyramid of spheres, 9, 8, and 7. Those individuals are not in charge of the beliefs they hold true, or of the goals they set for themselves. They make up the eighty-five percent (from the Five Percenters' philosophy) who are ignorant of their true identity. Once we recognize the flaws in our fundamental conditioning, we are ready to change. We begin to tap into the power of the sixth sphere, Heru, to lay down the platform of our individual belief system.

---

3   Mut, an Egyptian goddess whose name means "mother" was often represented wearing the vulture headdress. Not surprisingly, she became linked with the vulture because of her name. Vultures, with their extensive wingspan, were viewed as all-embracing protectors; in other words, mothers who give sheltering protection to children. Vultures were also seen as fierce defenders of their young. These strong maternal characteristics inspired the ancient Egyptians and were attributed to Mut, the ultimate motherly goddess. (http://classroom.synonym.com/significance-vultures-egyptian-headdresses-5610.html, 2001-2017, Leaf Group Ltd.)

The Story of Ausar

Like all systems of beliefs that provide people with a philosophical interpretation of life, the Tree of Life is rooted in a symbolical story which Ra Un Nefer defines as "metaphorein." This clarification emphasizes the significance of the story in a system of meditation aimed at promoting spiritual growth with the reawakening of energy dwelling in each sphere of the Tree itself. The Story of Ausar constitutes the central "metaphorein" for inspiration in the meditative reconnection with higher faculties. The Story tells of a time long ago in Kamit, when a king named Ausar achieved great prosperity for his land through spiritual cultivation.

Ausar's younger brother, Set, grew covetous of his sibling's success. With the help of his followers, Set conspired to kill the king and took over the empire. The rebels proceeded to cut up Ausar's body into fourteen pieces and threw them all over Kamit. Contrarily to his brother, the usurper of the Kamitian Kingdom ruled with violence and stopped spiritual cultivation throughout the land. He established a system of corruption, where he insidiously encouraged lavishness and lustful indulgence.

In the midst of such social degradation, Ausar's younger sisters, Auset and Neb Het,*[4] decided to look for their brother's body parts. They were successful in their quest. After they re-membered Ausar's body, they wrapped it in a white cloth and buried it at the bottom

---

4 Het Heru

of a river under the shield of the serpent, Kematef. The two sisters chanted and meditated during the whole process. Henceforth, Neb Het experienced an ecstatic state of trance, which reactivated Ausar's sexual ability to impregnate Auset with Heru.

When Set learned about the birth of his brother's son, he began a campaign to kill his nephew. Once Heru grew to adulthood, he decided to fight his uncle's violent rule. Just like his father, through meditation and under Tehuti's guidance, he succeeded in disarming Set and reclaiming his right to Kamit's throne. Subsequently, the new king managed to inspire his uncle in using the mastery of communication to spread Ausar's righteous philosophy all over the land and reinstate his legacy of spiritual cultivation.

A Path with a Heart

The Tree of Life as well as the Ausar's metaphorein constitute major tools in spiritual cultivation, not only for the Ausar Auset Society's members, but also for anyone who decides to acquire an expansive understanding of life. When I joined the AAS, my collective belief system was shattered. I was really feeling broken inside, still trying to reconcile the Five Percenters' view with Don Juan's teachings. My relationship with my husband was void of excitement. I had lost confidence about my understanding of life and myself as a woman. I devoted most of my time to my children's education. Nonetheless, my curiosity for Black culture and New Age spirituality grew stronger. This feeling within kept me hoping that one day I'd be free of the sadness and loss which characterized my life at that time.

My husband and I separated a few months after we joined the Ausar Auset Society. We attended workshops at the Philadelphia parish, which is closer to Trenton, New Jersey where we lived. The head priest of the community showed a great interest toward us. He openly encouraged my interest in the views of their spiritual leader, Ra Un Nefer Amen. His attention was flattering and boosted my female self-confidence. At first, my husband was very enthused about our membership with the group. However, when I became very involved in their activities, he didn't approve. I focused less on our conjugal issues. At one point it became evident that our relationship had reached a low and I had found an outlet that could shift my attention toward the healing of my inner dismay. My husband and I broke up without any divorce proceedings. He stopped his membership with the Ausar Auset community and I stayed.

I initiated a journey to acquire Ra Un Nefer Amen's teachings on his Tree of Life Meditation (TOLM) system. With great commitment and discipline, I learned to implement the techniques of Men Ab Em Aungk Em Maat by ignoring negative emotions such as anger and cravings for unhealthy foods. I adopted more sane habits like a strict vegetarian diet, fasting, Yoga, and the use of oracle systems, particularly the *I Ching*[5] for spiritual guidance and education. I attended and performed rituals that contributed to heal me from past experiences and awaken latent faculties inside of me. Meditations with the deity Auset helped me remember how strict my father was with me and how that affected my female joy and relationships with men. I also recollected how my mother used to treat me like a frail person who could easily be hurt. Those were hidden and painful memories. I had to go back to them to forgive my parents, and reclaim my Ausar identity. Chanting to Het Heru reconnected me with my female beauty and qualities. The monthly TOLM ceremonies constitute effective tools in the process of self-healing as well as finding appropriate solutions to external issues a person may face.

During the period I spent learning about the Ausarian system of philosophical thought, I encountered petty tyrants among fellow members from the Philadelphia community. For example, after my husband and I joined the AAS, I lent some audio tapes of Ra Un Nefer Amen's workshops at the headquarter in New York (which my sister shared with me, since she attended classes there) to some female parishioners of the Philadelphia local. I was not aware that sharing materials was against the society's protocols. Those items are inclusive of the organization's source of income. Therefore, members must purchase their own. Instead of orienting me to the code of behavior, those adept individuals reported the incident to the head priest, who in turn made me aware of the protocol while he was teaching a class. In another instance, after my separation from my husband, one of the single members from the group proposed that I sub rent from her, since I wanted to relocate to Philly with my children. Two or

---

5   *Book of Changes* in Chinese Culture, used as divination tool

three weeks before we moved in, she abruptly informed me that she had changed her mind. All the crossroads I experienced in the course of my association with the Ausar Auset Society did not wither my commitment to spiritual work.

When the time came to leave, circumstances in my life translated into omens indicating my probable separation from the group. One morning, my daughter was hit by a car right in front of the Ausar Auset Society's building in Philadelphia. Fortunately, her main injury was a broken tibia. Not long after that scarring incident, I was inducted into the high level of priesthood (Shekemship) in the society. Moreover, one day a young American woman came to visit the community. We discussed the organization's philosophy and upcoming events. When I told her I'm from Ayiti, she revealed to me that she was a member of Le Peristyle Haitian Sanctuary, a Voodoo church Gro Mambo Angela Novanyon created in Philadelphia during the 1980s. She also invited me to a ceremony that the group was holding at Penn State University later that month. I accepted her invitation, which I forwarded to both my sister, L., and my estranged husband. They travelled together to attend the event with me.

Another significant omen that convinced me of my imminent departure from the Ausar Auset Society took place during a workshop held by the parish head priest. He was delineating about Ausar's journey and his mummified body at the bottom of the river. As he was talking, I "saw" Ausar was alive in the depth of the body of water. I shared with the group that if our goal is to reach the first sphere of the Tree of Life, then it is really possible to awaken the energy dwelling within it. The spiritual facilitator did not entertain my position. Nonetheless, I could not deny the flash indicating the deity's resurrection in the river. Inside of me, I knew I had travelled the full length of my journey with the Ausar Auset Society.[6]

---

6   Essentially, spiritual development is a process of raising consciousness from the lower divisions of the spirit (the khaibit--sphere 10 and sahu—spheres 7. 8, 9) through the higher ones (spheres 6-1) to its original place"0" in the subjective realm. Once the individual has experienced the essential unconditionedness of his being, then he can live in the world in total freedom from all objective reality (not just simply the lower parts of being). (*Metu Neter Vol I* p. 139)

During the time I began to feel that I reached the end of my association with the Afrocentric group, my sister, L., had also outgrown her membership. We shared our thoughts apropos our inevitable separation from the group. We had never envisioned the time would come when we would leave the community where we, as well as our children, had developed caring friendships. We acquired valuable information and knowledge about spirituality. We learned about Kamit and its philosophical views regarding humanity. We experienced trance states, which stimulated our ability to transcend old conditionings and heal ourselves. We studied and worked on the use of oracle systems as tools for spiritual development. We shared special moments with fellow members. We also dedicated productive time to teachings, tie dying, and participated in other aspects of the daily activities of the organization.

Leaving the AAS after two years of intensive participation was not easy. However, both my sister and I knew the time had come to take back to the "Caldron" the fruit of our journey with the group. I personally consider the experience as having travelled a path with a heart.

"Anetch Hrak Mut, Atef, Neter
Ita Em Auset Ausar!"

V

THE RETURN OF HERU

1) Heru
2) The Catholic Experience
3) Voodoo

Heru

After I ended my membership with the Ausar Auset Society, I revisited the context of my collective belief system. Factors like limited financial means, my children's welfare, and the will to bounce back quickly on my feet pointed to my imminent return to the capital of New Jersey, a familiar location. I went back to live with my mother, my sister (who gave me shelter when I first came to the US), and her family. After my father passed away, my mom emigrated, and became a naturalized American citizen. My sister, L., and her family paid us frequent visits in New Jersey. The house became a center where our other siblings often converged and where our children bound joyfully with each other. Around that time, I reconciled with my husband. Subsequently, I enrolled at Mercer County Community College and obtained an Associate degree in Accounting.

I strove to maintain the foundation of my personal belief system (including The Mathematics, Don Juan's lessons, and the Ausarian views) in the milieu where I acquired the first ideas of my collective belief system. I meditated as often as I could. I fasted when the seasons changed. I even cooked some vegetarian dishes like barbecued tofu to encourage my non-vegetarian siblings to try a healthier diet. My sister L. also introduced the intake of supplements like Vitamins A, C, and E, as well as Acidophilus. Furthermore, I always kept the Mathematic of the day in mind. Castaneda's books remained easily accessible when I needed a source of serenity.

During the gathering of my family in New Jersey, everyone tended to act according to the old perception we had of each other.

Then and there, my eyes opened up to certain behavior patterns I demonstrated in the presence of my mother and my siblings. The former treated me as if I was a sickly and weak living being. Thus, the latter thought of me as a feeble person. Around them I was unsure of myself, always looking for their approbation. Memories of my childhood permeated my elation to reconnect with my family members.

When I was growing up in Ayiti, I think people pictured me as a runt. Petite and constantly reminded that I was powerless, I grew very timid. I was always "dans l'espace" too, as if I was trying to grasp some abstract reality. I was nonetheless academically brilliant. Everybody praised me for being a good student. I credit my father's diligence to tutor me when I started going to school. I was absent-minded at first. I also remember how much I prayed, and visualized to be the best student in my classes. Then, I applied myself to excel in every subject, including religion. When I was preparing for my First Communion, I mastered my Catechism so well that the school's principal suggested that I should join the convent. I didn't show any interest in becoming a formal servant to the Catholic Church. My parents didn't pressure me either to change my mind.

I had the opportunity to revisit my Catholic background after I went back to New Jersey. This journey also reinforced my Voodoo heritage. From my mother and my sisters, I learned about some counterparts of Voodoo spirits, or "Loas," to Catholic Saints. For example, St, Jacques, The Virgin Mary and Saint Patrick correspond to Ogou, Ezili, and Damballah, respectively. Author Maya Deren discussed this subject in *Divine Horsemen*, as well as author Karen McCarthy Brown in her *Mama Lola -A Voodoo Priestess in Brooklyn*. The former writes:

> Like the saints, the loas were once human and are the immediate guardians of the people. Like the saints, failing other images, the Voudoun serviteur today covers his altar with the Catholic pictures of the saints, which he understands as representations of the loa. (*Divine Horsemen*, p. 56)

Reconciliation

Voodoo (Voudoun) loas, Catholic saints, and Ausarian deities display common symbolisms. For example, St. Lazard is pictured as an old man at the entrance of a church. In Voodoo, Legba is the energy at the gate, just like the Ausarian Sebek at the crossroads. St. Patrick of the Christian is associated with snakes, similarly to Damballah of the Voodooist as well as the mummified Ausar guarded by the serpent Kematef. Incidentally, as I reconnected with my collective belief system, I began setting up my own shrines and performed rituals to invoke the energy linked to specific saints according to the Voodoo tradition.

At this point of my life, an interesting process started to unfold. I had brought back in the Caldron various perspectives, including the Five Percenters' views and Don Juan's lessons obtained from Castaneda's books. All those philosophies were brewing together to make up my personal belief system. After I returned to New Jersey to live with my family, I realized that Voodoo, its premise, and rituals encompass a cultural and genetic memory which transcends time. My mom and my sisters taught me about some Voodooist views and practices, but only to stimulate my intuition and connection to my ancestral legacy as well as to help me understand how much Voodoo focuses on people as energy.

The Voodoo perspective makes up an integral ingredient of my "Caldron," and is therefore an essential part of my personal belief system—one of its four corners. My return to New Jersey was inevitable. I had to claim my Voodoo heritage within the familial context. Indeed, the more I reconnected with my mom and siblings to experience our links to the loas, the more complete I felt. I knew that I was armed with all the attributes I needed to live a purposeful life. The Five Percenters' Mathematics, Don Juan's sobering lessons to his apprentice, my training with the Ausar Auset Society, and my ancestral spiritual roots provided me with a whole set of views to stop going on journeys for major perspectives regarding the meaning of life. I was no longer standing on my collective belief system. I had tapped into the sixth sphere of the Tree of life, Heru.

Heru is the hero in us. She only has choices of the heart to withstand battles against life challenges and challengers. I found myself inspired in all situations to stay above water, to curb reactions of self-importance, to remember Men Ab Em Aunghk Em Maat, and to catch the energy of the moment. Heru is the warrior inside of us who chooses to be free of patterns of thoughts and behavior she did not will. Among defeats and victories, she perseveres into this lonely path, where not many travel, because it implicates a fierce commitment to live truth. Often times testing situations emerge from people with whom she's emotionally involved such as family members and friends. Ultimately, it remains her choice to remember to breathe, to identify petty tyrants as challengers to her serenity, and to have faith in the path that keeps her heart light as a feather.

The Catholic Experience

With my new set of beliefs, I decided to revisit the Catholic Church. I began attending masses and observing some Christian holidays such as the Feast of St. John the Baptist on June twenty-fourth, the Feast of Our Lady of Mt. Carmel on July sixteenth, and of St. Patrick on March seventeenth. My decision was based on the clear understanding regarding the impact of a Christian education on the Ayisyen cultural legacy, Voodoo. The recognition that years of a systematic religious upbringing affect our basic behavior patterns results in a lucid assessment of our belief system: collective and personal.

When I reentered the steps of the Catholic churches, I bypassed the images of White saints to view them as female and male aspects of one energy. Then I could acknowledge the "numenous" dimension of religion, which author Ninian Smart evokes in *Worldviews, Cross cultural Explorations of Human Beliefs* (Third Edition). He cited the work of theologian Rudolph Otto, *The Idea of the Holy*, to support his discussion about religious experiences:

> For Otto, the 'numenous' experience is at the heart of religion. He defined it as the experience of something that is mysterium et fascinans—a mystery that is fearful, awe-inspiring (tremendum, literally meaning 'to be trembled at'). You get something of this feeling looking over a cliff. (*Worldviews*, p. 56)

According to Smart, the numenous experience can be stimulated through religious and ritualistic performances involving dimming of light, chanting, and singing as well as ringing bells.

One particular Sunday, I experienced the numinous dimension of religion during the rite of The Lord's Supper. Kneeling down, eyes closed, I listened to the cadenced voice of the priest reciting the Eucharistic prayer in the eerie silence of the church:

> *On the night he was given up for death,*
> *death he freely accepted,*
> *he took bread and gave you thanks.*
> *he broke the bread:*
> *gave it to his disciples, and said:*
> *Take this all of you, and eat it:*
> *This is my body which will be given up for you.*

At that moment, I felt Jesus's courage and his resolve to face his fate. Unanticipatedly, I heard the ringing of bells piercing the silence. I sank deeper into meditation, soaking in the remaining verses:

> *When supper was ended, he took the cup.*
> *again, he gave you thanks and praise,*
> *gave the cup to his disciples, and said:*
> *Take this all of you, and drink from it:*
> *This is the cup of my blood,*
> *The blood of the new and everlasting covenant.*
> *It will be shed for you and for all,*
> *So that sins may be forgiven.*
> *Do this in memory of me.*

During the Lord's Supper rite, my whole body experienced Jesus's passion and his readiness to cut off his own head for his beliefs in justice and righteousness. I understood instantly that the ritual prescribes how determined we, human beings must be in the face of crossroads, which test our commitment to truth. We must be willing to let go of erroneous ideas from our respective belief system and adamantly choose to cultivate a holistic way of life. We must be able to withstand

Ogou's (Heruhkuti's) purifying fire of justice to reach for Maat's truth.

My numenous experience with The Lord's Last Supper rite moved me to also attend The Stations of the Cross, a ceremony involving the walk through all the steps Jesus made on his way to the cross from the time he was sentenced to death to the moment he was buried. Catholics perform this ritual through the Lent period. During that time of year, they practice abnegation such as fasting, refraining from eating meat on certain days in preparation for the celebration of Jesus's Passion on Good Friday and his resurrection on Easter Day.

One Lent season, I applied myself to observe the celebration to its fullest. I attended all The Stations of the Cross rituals performed at the church where I became a member. My fervor helped me find the connection between the fourteen stations of the cross and the mutilation of Ausar's body into fourteen pieces. Those stations and pieces correspond to places that house emotions we must overcome to choose between self-importance and the commitment to realize peace within. The latter is not without pains and failures, but it is the Path with a Heart where we must find the courage to complete all the stations and claim the pieces of our true self to attain a state of detachment, void of self-importance. It is the road to self-liberation for a better understanding of life itself.

No one could teach me about my realizations from experiencing the Lord's Supper and The Station of the Cross rites with the standpoint of my personal belief system. I felt as though I completed an inner puzzle. In the Caldron, the ingredients started to come into one food that eventually will be offered to the Gods. I understood that instead of involving myself with an internal battle of rejecting my Catholic background, I must make peace with it and extricate the best part to strengthen my renewed way of seeing life. Effectively, in one instance I recalled Soeur (Sister) Germaine, the only model of peace and kindness I met during my years of Christian education. Another time, the words to the theme song at my First Communion ceremony came back to me. The content of this specific memory is significant to the subject matter of this book: reconciliation.

My classmates and I spent many weeks of preparation involving catechism classes, tests, and retreats until the day of our First

Communion. I was sick with a bad cold during the entire process, even on the day of the sacrament. Therefore, I went through the whole experience with a very collected disposition. I missed some lessons and had to attend a few one-on-one sessions with the nun in charge of the preparation. She was very impressed with my spiritual feedback. She suggested to my parents that I should join the convent, which I declined (as i previously mentioned).

The ceremony of my First Communion took place at the Cathedral[7] located in Port-au-Prince, the capital of Ayiti. The church was packed that sunny day of May. The long procession of young female communiants with their hands in a closed lotus mudra walked through the aisle singing the theme song (in French) until they found their seats:

Seigneur, Seigneur nous arrivons des quatre coins de l'horizon, dans ta maison.	(English Translation)
	O Lord, O Lord we've come from the four corners of the horizon, in your house.
Nous avons marché sur des routes diverses. Nous avons porté le fardeau des jours.	*We have walked on diverse roads.*
	We've carried our daily load.
Nous avons souffert la fatigue et la peine. Nous avons offert simplement notre amour.	*We've endured fatigue and pain.*
	We have offered simply our love.
Seigneur, Seigneur nous arrivons des quatre coins de l'horizon, dans ta maison.	*O Lord, O Lord we've come from the four corners of the horizon, in your house.*

The memory of my First Communion and the ritual's theme song provoked a continuous contemplative feeling within me, where I tried to make sense of my latest numenous experience in the Catholic Church. I knew I had dropped the Christian indoctrination of my collective belief system, where my educators taught me how to pray to a White God and his son Jesus and to believe blindly in religious tales. How then could I extricate valuable ingredients for my caldron from a religion that inherently conspires to reject my Voodoo heritage?

---

[7] The Cathedral was destroyed in the 2010 earthquake that rocked many parts of Ayiti.

Reconciliation

After weeks of contemplation concerning my Christian background, I found a key. Mystification is the bending of Truth. Catholicism rests on myths about God, his messengers, and the birth of his only son, Jesus. The stories are told in the Bible, which has been revised and translated over many years. The story of Eve and Adam, the first woman and man whom God placed in the Garden of Eden, undeniably represents one of the main tales in the Bible. According to the story, God instructed the couple to eat any fruit in the garden except for the apple. The snake convinced Eve to eat the forbidden fruit. In turn, the woman persuaded Adam to taste the apple. God proceeded to ban the couple from Eden, following their disobedience. What're Christians to do with such tale?

Catholic priests and religious leaders of other Christian denominations provide worshippers with various interpretations of biblical myths, but only to mystify and confuse them about the meaning of the stories and their origin. Truth must be twisted in the process of converting a people to a foreign set of religious beliefs. The African slaves must have realized that Christianity altered the versions of ancient stories from original cultures to institute its own religion+.[8]*
Therefore, it's not surprising that enslaved African priests and priestesses were able to merge images of White saints in their traditional rites without provoking any colons' brutal interdiction. Additionally, African and Native collaborated with each other to safeguard their spiritual beliefs and practices. Consequently, contemporary Ayisyen

---

8   The close ties between birth, the goodness of the gods, rebirth, and the image of the serpent infused Egypt during all of her early historical periods down to the end of the New Kingdom. When corn was harvested, and grapes pressed into wine, an offering was made to the harvest goddess, Thermuthis, who was depicted as either a snake or a woman with a serpent's head. Geb, the god of the earth and "the father of the gods," is referred to as "the father of snakes" that emerge from the earth. It is also significant, given Egyptian obsession with the quest for eternal life, that the snake "became a symbol of survival after death" (even resurrection) among the ancient Egyptians.

https://publications. mi. byu. edu/publications/. . . /S00007-50e5e94151cc-87Skinner.pdf

Serpent Symbols and Salvation in the Ancient Near East and the Book of Mormon. Andrew C. Skinner. Journal of Book of Mormon Studies 10/2 (2001): 42–55

Voodoo reflects aboriginal influence regarding some of their devotional rites. Ethnographer Maya Deren provides some references about the issue in Appendix B of her *Divine Horsemen*.

Voodoo

African and Native American slaves could experience the numinous dimension or simply trance states during their collaborative devotional rituals by invoking angels, deities, and higher forces according to their ancestral heritage. They used traditional instruments such as various kinds of drums to stimulate devotees' connection to the divine world. Their efforts to maintain the validity of their cultural roots led to a legacy of rhythms, chants, songs, and philosophical thoughts of ancient civilizations. Today, Ayisyens are fortunate to listen to traditional songs by Wawa & Racine Kanga, the late Azor, Dadou Pasquet, the late Manno Charlemagne, Syto Cave, Erol Josue… as well as bands like le Magnum Band, Boukman Experiens, and Boukan Ginen.

Voodoo remains at the heart of the collective belief system of every Ayisyen in spite of all the campaigns to suppress its institution as an organized religious group in Ayiti. Indeed, the Catholic Church and other Christian organizations like the Methodists and the Pentecotists have contributed to challenge the practice of Voodoo in the country. In his book, *Haiti – The Aftershocks of History*, author Laurent Dubois reports that during the US occupation of Ayiti, the marines instituted laws prohibiting Voodooist observances among Ayisyens. After the American colonization in the beginning of the 20th century, Ayisyen political leaders such as Stenio Vincent and Elie Lescot extended this religious persecution. Later, in the early 1940s, the Catholic Church as well as the Protestants reinforced the anti-Voodoo campaign on the land.

In addition to harassing crusades where many religious objects and sacred natural landscapes were destroyed, Voodoo endured also the wrath of racist scholars who contributed to promote voodoo phobia through definitions like hex, devilry, or delusive assumptions. They associate it to the practice of sordid rites no different than the subjective patterns of marketing to disseminate subliminal messages to a large population with the intent of influencing social trends and product consumption.

Fortunately, Voodoo has survived in the confines of Ayisyen families as an ancestral legacy that nourishes the sempiternal memory of our true origin. We are energy. This is the central theme of Voodoo: our understanding of life in terms of manifestations of energy. A Voodooist no doubt will be involved in ritualistic customs to invoke various aspects of one energy. Pouring libation, setting up shrines for the gods, chanting, and using colors, scents, and articles associated with specific deities are among ceremonial acts that can affect our environment. This way of life consistently demands that we examine the intentions of our hearts. Voodoo challenges us to wish upon others what we wish upon ourselves. When we stagnate in feeling of envy, hate, jealousy, and other weak and wicked emotions, we rather engage ourselves in somber attempts. We project destructive patterns of visualizations. Our intentions become rooted in personal gains to the detriment of the world and fellow humankind.

The basic premise of Voodoo, which stresses the understanding of ourselves in terms of energy (and its manifestations), duly endows us with mindfulness. This dowry includes a sense of responsibility to restrain the compulsion from emotions encapsulated in our collective belief system to emit heedless vibrations around us (in thoughts, words, and actions). The Voodooist aims at measuring the intentions of her heart before engaging herself in any life situation. She activates her will to ignore divisive, delusive and destructive feelings to promote conciliative and constructive emotions. This way, she's able to engage herself in spiritual, mental, and physical activities for the betterment of everyone and everything. Thus, she taps into higher faculties to perform miraculous deeds such as healing the sick, and why not changing water into wine.

Reconciliation

The return of Heru for the Ayisyen must encompass the understanding of Christian dogma on Voodoo. The journey to claim our personal belief system brings us back to our roots. It provides us with the lucidity to unveil the fog of mystification that engulfs our view of ourselves and our reality. The Truth never dies. Our heroic way back to our true essence reveals our will to stand on beliefs handing us tools that allow the progression towards a clear understanding of ourselves and life itself. Therefore, today I'm aware of the incidental clumping of my ancestral memory in Voodoo and my formal education in Catholicism. To diffuse this amalgam of perspectives, I involve not myself in an inner turmoil. I rather use the implements that I've acquired in my quest for a personal belief system, to dissipate the Christian confusion and further the purification of foods in the caldron.

VI

RECONCILIATION

1) The *I Ching*
2) Awareness: A Brief Discussion
3) Energy Channeling
4) Demystification

The *I Ching*

The Caldron, the fiftieth hexagram of the *Book of Changes* (the *I Ching*), revealed itself to me when I turned fifty. The *I Ching* constitutes one of the tools I acquired during my priesthood training with the Ausar Auset Society. Beside his own compendium of lectures on the philosophical content of this Chinese oeuvre, Ra Un Nefer Amen suggested author Richard Wilhelm's translation as well as *Astrology of I Ching* by W. K. Chu and W. A. Sherrill. In his introduction, Wilhelm defines the *I Ching* as "a collection of linear signs to be used as oracles." This system of divination uses straight and broken horizontal lines in series of threes (trigrams). Each of the eight trilinear figures that make up the body of the *I Ching* corresponds to a natural principle of life on earth. Following is a display of the various trigrams and their numerical designation within the structure:

	Upper Trigram							
Lower Trigram	1	34	5	26	11	9	14	43
	25	51	3	27	24	42	21	17
	6	40	29	4	7	59	64	47
	33	62	39	52	15	53	56	31
	12	16	8	23	2	20	35	45
	44	32	48	18	46	57	50	28
	13	55	63	22	36	37	30	49
	10	54	60	41	19	61	38	58

https://www.airesdecambio.com/ching-el-libro-de-las-mutaciones

The *I Ching* includes an organized set of 64 hexagrams, consisting of all the possible vertical arrangements of two trigrams (6 lines). Each hexagram is titled according to the image it reveals. An *I Ching* oracle reading is completed with the draw of two hexagrams. The idea of change is depicted with each line of the first hexagram leading up to an adjacent line in the second hexagram. *The Book of Changes* and its use of lines convey the concept of life as a scene of infinite possibilities.

The *I Ching* is a very intricate system of oracles. Whoever decides to acquire a true understanding about its relevance must not only study its schematic structure, but also undergo a spiritual training to awaken intuitive abilities for accurate interpretations of individual readings. This Chinese literary work can also be used as a source of wise inspirations. I often pick it up to tune my spirit when the need arises. Incidentally, The Caldron resurfaced in my mind at the appropriate age of fifty. It revealed its meaning and inspired me to write this book.

The Caldron is a very deep metaphorical notion. When we learn about various world views that potentially affect our perception of life, we must take the time to meditate on them. We must cook them in our caldron to purify our vision of the world and transform ourselves by rejecting fallacious beliefs in the process. Factually, the third edition of the Wilhelm/Baynes translation of the *I Ching* includes a forward by Swiss psychotherapist, Jung. He contends that "…the food (in the Caldron) is to be understood as spiritual nourishment." This big vessel holds spiritual beliefs. When those thoughts from our collective belief system fail to sustain our inner strength and our connection to the Divine, if we are true to ourselves, we must embark on a quest to find new aliments to build a personal system of beliefs.

Awareness

A Brief Discussion

Awareness encompasses the innate intelligence which enables us to acquire information, to comprehend, to become conditioned, to develop, and ideally, to improve our human condition on earth. It constitutes the malleable non-matter aspect of our being that our parents begin to mold from the time of our conception. Our awareness gradually takes the shape our first teachers (mother, father, guardians, relatives, siblings, academic and religious instructors, peers...) ascribed to it through lessons, guidance, and examples. This progressive conditioning results in the make-up of our collective belief system.

Hence, we gain membership in a society of people who share a common outlook on life: what is true or false, right or wrong, pretty or ugly... We learn how to think, act, and react. Individual experiences validate the reliability of accumulated notions in our collective belief system. When we fail to find effective answers or solutions to our inquiries, most of us remain blindly faithful to the values, the views, and the concepts we learned during the early stages of our life. Some of us attempt to search among worldviews from other (human) cultures for more fulfilling philosophical substances. We look for new teachers who can provide us with a more complete mold to our awareness. This phase of our existence involves effort to assume an individual belief system that would fundamentally equip us with effectual abilities to address the various challenges of our world.

The most auspicious way in the attempt to acquire other views inclusive to a more reliable definition of our reality is to humbly leave our collective belief system in the Caldron. Thereafter, we could proceed to picture ourselves going on a voyage with an empty suitcase, ready to collect awareness—enhancing aliments for the Caldron. This journey represents the travelling on paths that have heart, which Don Juan evokes in Castaneda's *A Yaqui Way of Knowledge*. We must not throw away our collective belief system nonetheless, since it constitutes one of the cornerstones of our individual belief system. What a paradox, indeed!

Ultimately, we will not know peace until we come across a perspective that emphasizes our essential being in terms of energy, including its various manifestations and its channeling within us. Once we reach such a path, we'll make connections to find answers from the source of knowledge itself. We'll tap into faculties that rely on the involuntary aspect of ourselves which Ra Un Nefer Amen discusses in *Metu Neter, Vol. 1*.

The Channeling of Energy

My recollection of the *I Ching*'s fiftieth hexagram coincided with an increasing desire to revisit the subject of *chakras*, or centers of energy. I first became exposed to the practice of *chakra* purification through breathing techniques during my priesthood training at the Ausar Auset Society. Evidently, the urge to learn more about the topic led me to pick up *The Serpent Power* by Arthur Avalon, a text that Ra Un Nefer Amen suggests to his followers. The book provides valuable information regarding the concept of *chakras*. The author presents background history on the topic, and educates the reader with the use of terms from the language of Ancient India (Sanskrit). Nonetheless, Avalon's technical style failed to satiate the sudden thirst that compelled me to acquire a deeper understanding in respect to energy channels.

I decided to look for other sources about the subject. In an issue of One Spirit, a catalog that distributes books on spirituality, *Chakra Meditation* by Swami Sarananda caught my attention. I decided to order it from the vendor. The literature and illustration of this work became additional and essential tools to the purifying conduction in the Caldron.

In *Chakra Meditation*, Sarananda discusses the notion of *chakra* in a "friendly user" way. The reader can easily familiarize himself to the role energy channels play in the physical body. The text describes in simple terms the flow of life force within people, and how it relates to a balanced life. Vital energy is distributed inside us through channels, or *nadis* for the Chinese. *Nadis* intersect at points called *chakras* (major and minor). The flow of energy in the *nadis* compares to the circulation of blood in the veins and other inner vessels. Thus, we must adopt healthy habits to avoid blockage in those channels (*nadis*) just like we must prevent any clot in our blood vessels and all organs in the circulation system. For example, blood distribution in the physical body involves the function of veins, arteries, valves…including the lungs, which are defined as "a pair of organs in the chest that supplies the body with oxygen and removes carbon dioxide from the body."[9] Therefore, we must keep our lungs clear of impurities for proper blood flow within us just as we must ensure the cleansing of the *nadis* and the *chakras* for the fluid course of our life force in the physical body.

Chakra Meditation provides breathing techniques as well as Yoga poses that contribute to the harmonious distribution of energy in the *nadis*. All these practices compare to the continuous stirring movement that results in the tune-up of the channels constituting the path through which our vital energy circulates. Additionally, the book includes meditations aimed at controlling or regulating the release of energy in the *chakras*. Without a clear understanding of the distribution of energy within us as well as an implementation of techniques that maintain the harmonious conduction of vital force in our body, the views in the Caldron would lead to separate notions we can merely talk about. We would at times experience hunches about events in our environment without developing any permanent change in our behavior patterns.

Most of us grow up learning about human anatomy and physiology. We study the physical make-up of our body in terms of its components and their functions. These learned concepts provide us with a limited scope concerning our human existence on earth. They fail to educate us about the inward force that animates us and allows us to exist in the physical realm. This vibrance is our life, the gift the Creator entrusts to us. We must oversee its sustainability with the knowledge of energy channeling if we want to achieve wholistic health and inner stability.

---

[9] https://www.ncbi.nlm.nih.gov/pubmedhealth/PMHT0023062

People who devote themselves to enhanced spiritual development come across practices such as *Tai Chi*[10] and *Qigong*.[11] *Chi* or *Qi* translates to vital energy in Chinese. Therefore, those two disciplines address the healthy flow of Chi in the physical body. Effectively, in the introduction of *Chakra Meditation* (p. 19), Swami Sarananda writes:

> Ancient Chinese traditions share some of the concepts we use in chakra meditation: *prana,* Sanskrit for subtle energy, is referred to in Chinese philosophy as *chi* or *Ki,* and what are known as the *nadis* or energy channels in the Indian tradition are 'meridians' in the Chinese model.

Nadis intersect at points called *chackras* which respectively house the qualities of earth, water, fire, air, and ether. The different aspects of energy permutate within these five elements from points to points. For example, one quality of earth is solidity; of water is fluidity; of fire is transformation like (water into vapor); of air is lightness; of ether is boundlessness. As our life force travels through the *nadis* to reach the *chakras,* our habits, activities, environment, people, and events around us affect its motion. Therefore, we must study and observe the natural laws that govern this dynamic upward and downward centric flow to gain *awareness* of this inner force that moves us. We must take charge of it. This inquiry can also teach us the way to handle our *chi* under the pressure of our way of life.

Our emotions change from one state to another once they meet at the *chakras*. When we clear the *nadis* with exercises like *Tai Chi* and *Qi Gong*, we allow our life force to flow harmoniously within ourselves. The way to look within to take control of our adverse sentiments (envy, lust, jealousy, hate, covetousness...) is with self-inquiry exercises such as meditation. These personal surveys open our spirit to learn directly

---

10, 10 Tai chi and qi gong are centuries-old, related mind and body practices. They involve certain postures and gentle movements with mental focus, breathing, and relaxation. The movements can be adapted or practiced while walking, standing, or sitting. In contrast to qi gong, tai chi movements, if practiced quickly, can be a form of combat or self-defense. (Tai Chi and Q Gong: in Depth /NCCIH https://nccih.nih.gov/health/taichi/introduction.htm, *October 2016*) https://nccih.nih.gov/health/taichi/introduction.htm, *October 2016*)

from the Divine Intelligence. Author Ninian Smart writes about this state of attainment in *Worldviews*:

> There is another kind of religious experience—mystical experience—that has been very important to the history of humanity, and that does not seem to have the qualities Otto ascribes to the numinous. Thus, in the Indian tradition particularly and especially in Buddhism, we find the practice of Yogic meditation, aimed at purifying the consciousness of the individual to such a degree that all images and thoughts are left behind. It is as if the meditator is ascending a kind of inner ladder where at the highest rungs he or she gains a kind of bliss and insight, free from the distractions of ordinary experience. (*Worldviews*, p. 58)

Our body comprises minor and major *chakras*. More *nadis* interconnect with the latter, thus the distinction from the former. Minor *chakras* are located in points such as the palms of our hands, the soles of our feet, and our shoulders. Major *chakras* are aligned on the central *nadis* located near the spine area. They include: the root *chakra*, the water *chakra*, the solar plexus, the heart *chakra*, the throat *chakra*, the brow *chakra,* and the crown *chakra*. Following is a brief discussion on the major centers of energy housing the main manifestations of the five elements.

The root chakra corresponds to the Caldron and its content of beliefs (collective and individual). These resides our sense of grounding within the earth element. The water chakra houses qualities such as fluidity and creativity. Under the influence of this center of energy, the mix of ideas in the Caldron can flow in a liquid/flexible state in preparation for change. These two lower chakras connect and meet to complete the pyramid of our belief system (collective and individual). This point of connection correlates with the energy that stands at the gate, Sebek or Legba, to test our willingness to change as well as our readiness to sustain the heat from the next center of energy.

The Hindu calls the chakra at the solar plexus (around the navel area) "Manipura," or city of shining jewels. It houses the energy of the fire element. The function of this chakra is to transform the ideas in their fluid state into the winds of possibility. It takes a lot of energy to alter fundamental patterns of behavior dictated by our collective belief system. The process of energy channeling eases the diastolic and systolic movements within, which generate the fire power to change our views and transform ourselves. This transmutation progresses to the heart chakra, which holds the qualities of the air element.

The energy at the solar plexus supports our ability to choose. Indeed, it takes fire power to will a change in behavior patterns. Otherwise, we stagnate in old ways that don't stimulate our faculty to rise above the fallacies in our collective belief system. To withstand the heat from challenges to overcome, we must be heroic. We must own our heart and be passionate to let the fire from the Manipura chakra purify our vision of the world. Then, we'll be able to let go of erroneous beliefs and choose the Truth.

When we tie the subject of chakras to the Tree of Life, we recall the process of transcendence that leads to Men Ab (Keeping the heart still), the attribute of the Kamitian deity, Maat. She completes the interplay between the solar plexus and the heart chakras. Maat is adequately depicted as a female deity holding a scale measuring a heart against the lightness of a feather.

Earth and water have been transformed by fire into vapor (air). This statement symbolizes the ability to change and overcome old behavior patterns that are detrimental to our well-being.

At this point, we may infer that:

1. Our life force (energy) flows through channels called *nadis*.
2. We must learn about ways to purify the *nadis*.
3. When we cleanse the *nadis*, energy flows easily inside us.
4. *Nadi*s intersect at centers of energy called *chakras* (minor and major)
5. More *nadis* intersect at major *chakras*.
6. The seven major *chakras* are aligned down the spine area.
7. Through self-inquiry such as meditation, we become involved in the process of equalizing units of energy inside the centers of energy.

8. Each *chakra* will eventually house the right amount of energy through transmutation.

When energy does not flow properly inside of us, our *chakras* may contain too little or too much energy. We could accumulate all the wonderful ideas in the world and aspire to change ourselves and our environment. We find ourselves still searching until we learn to define ourselves in terms of energy. Once we're able to cleanse the channels of energy and balance the amount of energy within the *chakras*, we activate dormant faculties that bring about the ability to learn directly from the source of Knowledge. This statement leads to the discussion about the three remaining centers of energy—the throat, the brow, and the crown *chakras*.

The effort to cleanse the nadis and maintain the equal distribution of life force in the chakras requires a great deal of discipline, constant work of the will, and unbending resolve to awaken our godly potential. The achievement of the Men Ab Em Aunghk Em Maat state creates a feeling of detachment…from our collective belief system. The throat chakra holds the energy of the element, ether where lie all possibilities. When we finally tap into this center of energy, we're considering the potential to express and manifest our individual beliefs. We're contemplating the possibility to affect the world constructively by inspiring others in the sense of impregnating them with the energy to move towards Kindness in behavior.

The continuous struggle to ignore the thoughts from our collective belief system and choose to apply the notions from our personal system of beliefs not only empowers us to actively promote a balanced way of life around us, but also gradually stimulates our ability to intuit and to hear the soft voice of knowledge. The brow *chakra* consists of such center of energy. About it, the author of *Chakra Meditation* writes:

> If the flow of energy at your ajna chakra is healthy, your mind is focused and you are blessed with a vivid, yet disciplined, imagination. You are likely to be charismatic, Highly intuitive, unattached to material possessions, and possibly prone to experience Psychic phenomena.

When we reach this state of being, we've become wise and ready to achieve the state of inner peace as we keep cleansing our channels of energy and meditating on the *chakras*.

The seventh major *chakra* constitutes the seat of enlightenment. No specific element is linked to this center, since it equates to the transcendence of our attachment to the material world, and conveys the achievement of our essential identity in Peace. The meaning of our existence in the physical world is to become so detached from the mundane aspect of life with invigorating practices until we succeed to manifest our god-like nature on earth. After we unlock our crown chakra, we draw knowledge directly from the undifferentiated creative source. The throat, the brow, and the crown chakras make up the last major pyramid within us. This area comprises the harness of energy to reach our natural endowment of Grace, Enlightenment, or Nirvana.

Balancing the energy inside the *chakras* requires discipline, dedication, and commitment. We must convince ourselves this defines our main life objective and we can consciously affect the flow of energy inside us. The process of attaining nirvana consists of a viable journey, which involves the purification of beliefs (the solid matter from the Earth chakra or the Caldron) as well as the channels through which our life force (energy) travels. This cleansing involves an upward movement starting with our concession that our collective belief system is flawed. It continues with our decision to seek for new thoughts that will inspire us to complete the first pyramid of our personal set of beliefs.

The course of our transformation reaches a second level once we find the courage to stand for what we believe and grow more and more passionate about it. This resoluteness will eventually lead us to the gate where we will acquire the awareness of ourselves in terms of energy and live our life accordingly. Thus we'll relegate the voice of reason in its place and begin to tap into the third pyramid of faculties encompassing higher faculties such as omnipotence, omniscience, and omnipresence. There, we will offer the purified set of beliefs to the gods. Once we achieve the ability to learn from the Creative Source, this power (energy) begins flowing down the chakras to the bottom of the Caldron (the Earth Chakra), where it coils itself as the process of transformation repeats itself until the attainment of Enlightenment or Nirvana.

Demystification

The delineation of the enlightenment process can help debunk some religious concepts and lift their fog of mystification in the world. The religious construct of most people's collective belief system uses myths to describe humanity's inner or spiritual reality. Those stories find their origin in ancient cultures such as those of Kamit and Ancient India, where spirituality involved tales about spheres of energy and their manifestations. Modern religions are engaged in a process of mystification through countless translations and explanations of old texts. This indoctrination is contrary to humanity while concealing people's true goal on earth.

Metaphorically, enlightenment constitutes the food in the Caldron that will be offered to the Creator. After we pour in the Caldron views that impact our awareness towards an individual belief system, and when we become involved in energy channeling practices, our understanding of the world becomes heightened. We progressively acquire the ability to learn from the Creative essence. We begin to define ourselves in terms of energy, putting the voice of reason in its place. Subsequently, a process of transformation develops within us. The Caldron, the most natural receptacle of ideas, stores the purified views we acquire from the Highest Source of Knowledge. This accumulation of enlightening views, transformed as energy, stores itself in a spiraling fashion at the bottom of the Caldron the more inspiration we acquire. In the Hindu tradition, the purified knowledge in the Caldron is defined as a feminine divinity, Kundalini. At the time of enlightenment, the Goddess uncoils herself and rises to the crown chakra to produce a beautiful firework of lucidity and happiness through our body.

In the Christian context, the notion of enlightenment is twisted, which leads to the mystification of the adept and the novice worshippers. This assessment is evident not only in a textual form, but also in pictorial displays. Effectively, Catholics especially worship the image of the Virgin stepping on a serpent's head. She's titled: "Our Lady of Grace." Today, a basic electronic search about the depiction's meaning reveals people's confusion on the subject. Many individuals think that it symbolizes the Virgin Mary's victory over the devil. Some fancy about the translation of the text (Genesis 3:15) in the Bible (from Hebrew to English) rendering the mythology. Evidently, Genesis, the first book of the Old Testament (of the Christian Bible) planted the image of the serpent as the devil within us. Indeed, the myth of Eve and Adam in the Garden of Eden narrates how the serpent deceives the couple into eating the forbidden fruit. This tale lays the foundation for Christianity to perpetuate the conception regarding the serpent as the evil within us.

The serpent is not the devil. The Serpent represents the coiling shape of the knowledge (Truth) we acquire from the Creative Source and the Sinuous Path it travels in the process of Enlightenment. The Apple symbolizes the Knowledge accumulated in the Caldron, which will rise until we succeed in energy channeling by purifying the nadis and balancing the chakras. Plainly, Eve in a serpentine path brought the Apple to Adam, not out of disobedience, but to accomplish the true objective of people on earth: Nirvana.

The dissipation of the fog from Christian mystification also involves the signification of two Catholic celebrations: The Feast of Ascension and The Feast of Assumption. The former is celebrated forty days after Easter Sunday*[12] to commemorate Jesus's induction into heaven. Many Christians observe the Feast of Assumption on August fifteenth to hail Mary's arrival into paradise. Young and old believers attempt to decipher the difference between the two words.

---

12 The day Christians celebrate Jesus' resurrection

Most agree that Jesus ascended on his own, while Mary was raised into heaven. These interpretations fail to provide congregations with a perspective that will help them find their way to the truth. They only deepen devotees' confusion about the value of these symbolic holidays.

Religious institutions succeed in confusing their faithful members with doctrines that distort the Truth concerning the essential nature of people as vessels of energy. Indeed, the attribution of the Feast of Ascension to a male deity, and that of the Feast of Assumption to a female deity is accurate. Nonetheless, the catechistic precepts behind these celebrations are fallacies which perpetuate the misleading of parishioners regarding their true connection to the spiritual world.

The devotional and solemn settings of religious services with candles, bells, images of saints, canticles, rows of chairs or benches with breviaries on them... provoke the numinous experience within attendees. In addition to the décor, the evangels and the sermons refuel members' enthusiasm, which reinforces their faith and their belief system. Those whose earth chakra is more vibrant, grow fervently touched by the setting. Those whose water chakra is gorged with fluid energy become animated and stimulate the numinous experience among participants.

At the end, everybody is aroused with ideas that redirect their mental process to the common religious beliefs they hold true. This ephemeral state of euphoria closes the way to spiritual elevation. Incidentally, a Christian sermon would no way reveal that the Feast of Ascension is related to Jesus, because it takes fire (associated to a male energy) to transform Into light the colled Knowledge In the Caldron (Kundalini, a female deity) and lift her to the crown chakra for enlightenment. Eventually, parishioners will not celebrate the feasts of male and female fusion of energy to offer the purified food in the Caldron to the Creator.

The image of the Virgin stepping on the serpent's head is connected to the story of Adam and Eve, to the Feasts of Ascension and Assumption as well as to many other Christian myths. It translates into the human primordial responsibility to cultivate our awareness by searching for Truth while nurturing the flow of energy inside us. We must claim this Knowledge, (it is our true goal). Stepping on the serpent's head means that we own it (this knowledge). We must believe and affirm the grip on our life journey on paths that have heart until we generate enough energy to bring manifest the Light within in the physical world.

CONCLUSION

This book does speak about my personal experience of reconciliation. The journey has brought me back to my collective belief system where my first outlook on life, as well as the confusion about my true goal on earth, have taken root, sprouted, and sprung up. I have evoked Christian ideas to describe mystification as it pertains to my own religious background. To readers who find inspiration in this book, and whose religion is other than Christianity, the distortion of Truth will unfold according to their respective indoctrination. Reconciliation is an individual quest that leads to the understanding of ourselves in terms of energy.

Many behavior patterns are intrinsic to our cultural upbringing: the language(s) we speak; the food we eat; the clothes we wear; certain traits of conduct (reflecting ancestral adaptation to the environment) that we've preserved. All this encompasses genetic memories which at time preclude our awareness of the present world. The natural connection I sense with Voodoo and the mystical experience it provokes inside of me illustrate probable recollection of past spiritual journeys. Therefore, as we progress in our reconciliation quest, we remain anchored in our collective belief system. We do not hold the power to undo certain elements of behavior such as the language we speak or our affinities to certain foods or musical rhythms. However, some individual memories of previous inner passages take over in actual time when the appropriate environmental conditions are met to bring about this state of self-discovery.

After I had left Ayiti, I entered the US not only with my travelling documents and my luggage of personal items, but also with the baggage of my collective belief system. Not too long after, the content of ideas characterizing my behavior began to feel like an outdated wardrobe. The way I learned to view the world up to my teen years did not equip me to adapt to the fast pace of the American culture, its egotistic mindset, and its densely diverse population. I lost certainty in the beliefs that I had carried for many years as guidelines for proper behavior. I longed to regain control of my thought process.

The Five Percenters' premise that the Black man is God gave a magnificent jolt to my vision of myself and the world. The desire to change prepares a person to accept the challenge to learn new ideas. When I lost faith in my collective belief system, I also stopped believing in the White God I learned about. I embraced Clarence 13X's teachings. They shifted my awareness to the conviction that I am not an inferior human being and brought me closer to the divinity within me, just as it should be for everybody. However, all Black people must hear the statement that the Black man is God. The widespread image of a White God has caused his non-white worshipers to move away from the belief that they were too conceived in the image of the Creator.

Once we free our minds of the chains that restrict us from connecting with the Divine energy, our awareness opens itself to other edifying perspectives. Incidentally, after I read Don Juan's statement about the travelling on paths that have heart, I became so entrenched in Castaneda's tutelage that Don Juan's teachings became elementary to my individual belief system.

Furthermore, the Native Americans' wisdom and its standpoint that self-importance is our biggest enemy can captivate the attention of anyone seeking to transcend old behavior patterns. Certainly, other sages provide resources that inspire humility. This sort of teaching motivates us to search for beneficial exercises that further our spiritual development. We eventually feel compelled to practice the new notions we learn to assess the change in our behavior.

My membership with the Ausar Auset Society significantly

contributed to the spiritual development that equips me to take charge of my thought process, my utterances, my feelings, and my actions. I believe that the Ausarian experience and the achievement of the Ausar Em Aunghk Em Maat compare to the process of fighting self-importance as Don Juan prescribes. With great discipline, I completed my priesthood training. I learned about the Tree of Life, meditation, breathing techniques, the I Ching, Chakras, and other spiritual concepts. When it was time for me to leave, I saw the signs, and knew that I had travelled the full length of my journey with the Ausar Auset Society. As we engage fully on the quest to acquire new beliefs, we become disciples of different schools of thoughts. One important lesson we learn is to acknowledge omens on our path indicating the appropriate course of actions to follow.

I never thought that I would go back to the replicated setting where I learned the first elements of my collective belief system. My mom and my siblings could not see me with different eyes. However, I returned among them according to the scheme of my journey to seal my individual belief system. I had to cleanse myself of the fallacies in my collective belief system. Often time, we absorb ourselves in an inner conflict with the ideas we've acquired from our first teachers. We take drastic actions to reject those notions. However, we turn in circles without transcending old behaviors or transforming ourselves. Therefore, we must strive to take the best part from everything. With such disposition, we'll understand that we need to look inside and scrub wrong collection of ideas off our learned behavior. Thus, we'll start to extract traumatic memories in addition to erroneous views we carried all our lives. This way back takes us home, to move us closer to the center of ourselves.

The physical conditions were met for the reunion between me and my blood relatives. Above all, it entailed recollecting the dynamics of our relationship with each other as well as understanding some of my patterns of behavior. I know mom and my siblings will always see me and treat me like I'm still the same person from before I began the journey to claim my individual belief system. This constitutes one of the ramifications of people's collective belief system. On the other hand, I went back home to claim my ancestral heritage in Voodoo. I know now that voodoo rests on the philosophy that people are energy. Therefore, fundamentally, the true Voodooist must always weigh the intentions of her or his heart in every situation, especially in devotional contexts. Ultimately, Voodoo is a path with a heart.

For an Ayisyen, the practice of Voodoo involves a parallel with Catholicism, considering the campaign of Christianization missionaries accomplished during slavery times in the Americas. I also had to revisit the Catholic Church, especially to question why Voodoo still uses the pictures of White saints to depict the loas. This inquiry helped me recall the experience of my first communion and examine this major feature in my collective belief. Thereupon, I realized the meaning of mystification. I recognized that to lose or mislead an individual, a purporting party must use a way, a concept, or an idea familiar to that person and entwines it out of shape. I knew that at this point, I had sealed the platform of my individual belief system. I just had to persevere in the usage of the tools I acquired from the time I heard the Black man is God.

Following my studies of the Five Percenters' philosophy, the teachings of Don Juan, Ra Un Nefer Amen, and Voodoo reminded me that people are energy. During my priesthood training with the Ausar Auset Society, I learned about chakras, meditation, breathing techniques, divination, and other holistic concepts. I had to keep implementing the teachings that helped build my individual system of beliefs. It took many years for people to convince us of the world external reality. It's going to take the rest of our life to keep the connection with the inner reality of our being. We must be passionate in the understanding that we are energy. Our goal consists in the transformation of ourselves through the science of energy channeling, which involves the cleansing of nadis as well as practices like meditation to balance centers of energy or chakras.

Once we identify with our essential nature in energy, we become in touch with the intelligence that guides its course. We all have inside of us a receptacle that holds our views about life. When we examine (meditate on) them, we become involved in a cleansing process for insight. This is our dialogue with the Higher Intelligence, where we gradually learn the true meaning of our journey in the world involving a thorough assessment of our beliefs. This Truth will be stored in the Caldron, The Holy Grail of Reconciliation. It will coil itself at the bottom of our inner receptacle the more knowledge we acquire, and the more perseverance we demonstrate in energy channeling. The Christian image of The Lady of Grace stepping on the serpent's head, as well as the Serpent's Kematef protecting Ausar's dead body at the bottom of the river in the Kamitian Story of Ausar, symbolize the way we must nurture and protect the Truth until the time we achieve inner peace to claim the crown of Enlightenment.

BIBLIOGRAPHY

Castaneda Carlos, *The Teachings of Don Juan: A Yaqui Way of Knowledge*, Pocket Books, New York, 1968
    The Fire from Within, Pocket Books, New York, 1985

Deren Maya, *Divine Horsemen*, Mc Pherson & Company, New York, 1983

Dubois Laurent, Haiti, *The Aftershocks of History*, Picador, New York, 2013

Ra Un Nefer Amen, *Metu Neter, Vol. 1*, Khamit Corp., New York, 1990

Sarananda Swami, *Chakra Meditation*, Duncan Baird Publishers Ltd, UK and USA, 2008

Smart Ninian, Worldviews, *Crosscultural Explorations of Human Beliefs, 3rd Edition*, New Jersey, 1995, 2000

Wilhelm Richard/Baynes Cary, *The I Ching or Book of Changes*, Bollingen Foundation Inc, New Jersey, 1967

Further Reading:

Brown Dan, *The Da Vinci Code*, DOUBLEDAY, New York, 2003

www.ingramcontent.com/pod-product-compliance
Lightning Source LLC
Chambersburg PA
CBHW052103070526
44584CB00017B/2313